Cambridge IGCSE® Biology

Practice Book

Dave Hayward

Answers can be found at www.hodderplus.com/igcsebiology.

The publishers would like to thank the following for permission to reproduce copyright material.

Photo credits

p.133 © Jeremy Burgess / Science Photo Library

Questions from the Cambridge IGCSE Biology papers are reproduced by kind permission of Cambridge International Examinations.

This text has not been through the Cambridge endorsement process.

Hachette UK's policy is to use papers that are natural, renewable and recyclable products and made from wood grown in sustainable forests. The logging and manufacturing processes are expected to conform to the environmental regulations of the country of origin.

Orders: please contact Bookpoint Ltd, 130 Milton Park, Abingdon, Oxon OX14 4SB. Telephone: (44) 01235 827827. Fax: (44) 01235 400454. Lines are open 9.00–5.00, Monday to Saturday, with a 24-hour message answering service. Visit our website at www.hoddereducation.com.

© Dave Hayward 2013
First published in 2013 by
Hodder Education, an Hachette UK Company,
338 Euston Road
London NW1 3BH

Impression number   5 4 3 2 1
Year   2016 2015 2014 2013

All rights reserved. Apart from any use permitted under UK copyright law, no part of this publication may be reproduced or transmitted in any form or by any means, electronic or mechanical, including photocopying and recording, or held within any information storage and retrieval system, without permission in writing from the publisher or under licence from the Copyright Licensing Agency Limited. Further details of such licences (for reprographic reproduction) may be obtained from the Copyright Licensing Agency Limited, Saffron House, 6–10 Kirby Street, London EC1N 8TS.

Cover photo © Steve Knell / Nature Picture Library
Typeset in Frutiger 55 Roman 9 points by Datapage (India) Pvt. Ltd.
Printed and bound by the MPG Printgroup, UK
A catalogue record for this title is available from the British Library

ISBN 978 1444 18045 9

Contents

1 Characteristics of living organisms — 1

2 Classification of living organisms — 6

3 Using simple keys — 12

4 Cell structure and organisation — 15

5 Levels of organisation — 19

6 Diffusion and active transport — 24

7 Osmosis — 30

8 Enzymes — 35

9 Nutrition and nutrients — 39

10 Plant nutrition — 43

11 Human diet — 48

12 Digestion and absorption — 51

13 Transport in plants — 57

14 Transport in humans — 61

CONTENTS

15 Respiration — 68

16 Excretion in humans — 73

17 Reactions to stimuli by plants and invertebrates — 77

18 Coordination and response — 81

19 Reproduction, growth and development in plants — 87

20 Reproduction, growth and development in animals — 93

21 Inheritance — 99

22 Variation — 104

23 Energy flow, food chains and food webs — 109

24 Nutrient cycles — 114

25 Population size — 118

26 Human influences on the ecosystem — 121

Past exam questions — 125

1 Characteristics of living organisms

1 Draw lines to match each characteristic of living organisms to its definition.

Characteristic	Definition
nutrition	the breakdown of food in cells to release energy
respiration	an increase in size, mass and complexity of an organism
excretion	producing offspring, which prevents extinction of the species
sensitivity	this involves feeding – obtaining nutrients for growth, energy and maintaining health
reproduction	in response to changes, e.g. presence of a predator, to find food or a mate
growth	the ability to detect changes in the surroundings
movement	getting rid of the waste products made by chemical reactions in cells

(7 marks)

2 Mnemonics are used to remember lists of terms, e.g. 'Richard of York gave battle in vain' is used for the order of colours of the rainbow. Make your own sentence of seven words to remember the characteristics of life.

....

....(3 marks)

3 Complete the crossword puzzle about the characteristics of life, using the clues to help you.

Across

5 getting rid of the waste products made by chemical reactions in cells (9)

6 involves feeding – obtaining nutrients for growth, energy and maintaining health (9)

7 the breakdown of food in cells to release energy (11)

Down

1 the ability to detect changes in the surroundings (11)

2 producing offspring, which prevents extinction of the species (12)

3 in response to changes, e.g. presence of a predator, to find food or a mate (8)

4 an increase in size, mass and complexity of an organism (6)

(7 marks)

4 Complete the table by naming **two** excretory products made by plants and **two** excretory products made by animals. Name the processes that produce them.

Organism	Product	Process
plant	1	
	2	
animal	1	
	2	

(8 marks)

Stretch and challenge

5 Distinguish between respiration and breathing.

....

....

....

.... (4 marks)

6 Explain why biologists do not accept defecation as an example of excretion.

....

.... (2 marks)

■ *Exam focus*

1 Which characteristic is shown first when an earthworm is pecked by a bird? Circle the letter of the correct answer.

  A respiration
  B sensitivity
  C excretion
  D movement   [1]

2 The diagram shows a cow.

The cow is observed over a number of hours. State **three** observations that could be made to show that the cow is a living organism.

1 ....

2 ....

3 .... [3]

3 A car is non-living, but shows some characteristics which are also observed in living things.

  (a) State **two** characteristics that the car has in common with living things.

  1 ....

  2 .... [2]

  (b) State **two** characteristics of living things that a car does not show.

  1 ....

  2 .... [2]

  [Total: 4]

4 The diagram shows a bacterium. It demonstrates a number of the characteristics of living things such as reproduction, movement and respiration.

Name **three** other characteristics of living things that you would expect the bacterium to show.

1 ....
2 ....
3 .... [3]

2 Classification of living organisms

1 Complete the table by naming each of the kingdoms of organisms described. The first has been done for you.

Kingdom	Description
animal	Multicellular organisms that have to obtain their food. Their cells do not have walls.
	Single-celled, with a nucleus. Some have chloroplasts.
	Many are made of hyphae, with nuclei and cell walls (containing chitin), but no chloroplasts.
	Multicellular organisms with the ability to make their own food through photosynthesis, due to the presence of chlorophyll. Their cells have walls (containing cellulose).
	Very small and single-celled, with cell walls, but no nucleus.

(4 marks)

2 For each of the animals shown below:

(a) name the invertebrate group to which it belongs

(b) state **two** features, visible in the diagram, which put it in this group.

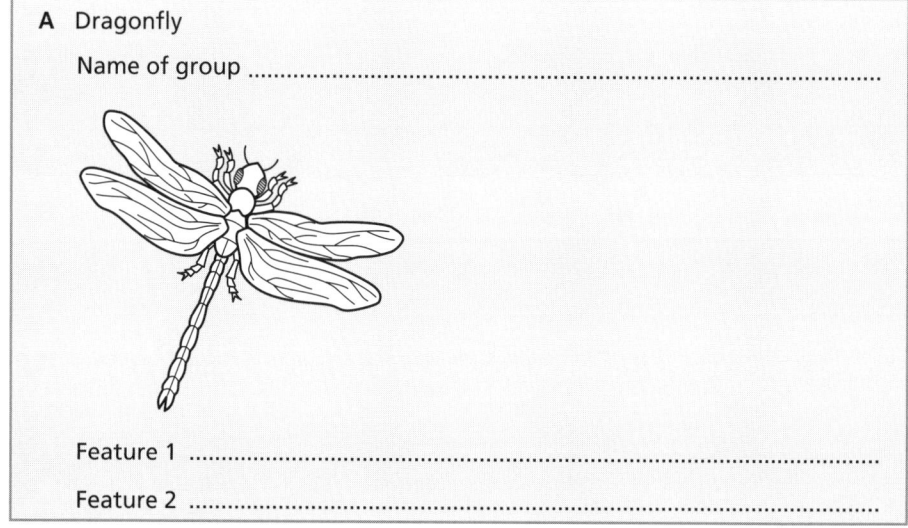

A Dragonfly

Name of group ....

Feature 1 ....
Feature 2 ....

B Earthworm

Name of group ....

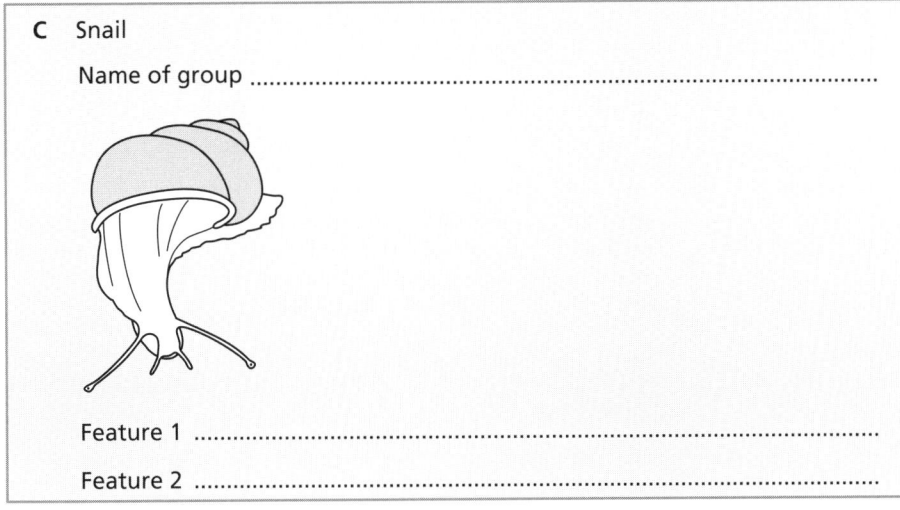

Feature 1 ....

Feature 2 ....

C Snail

Name of group ....

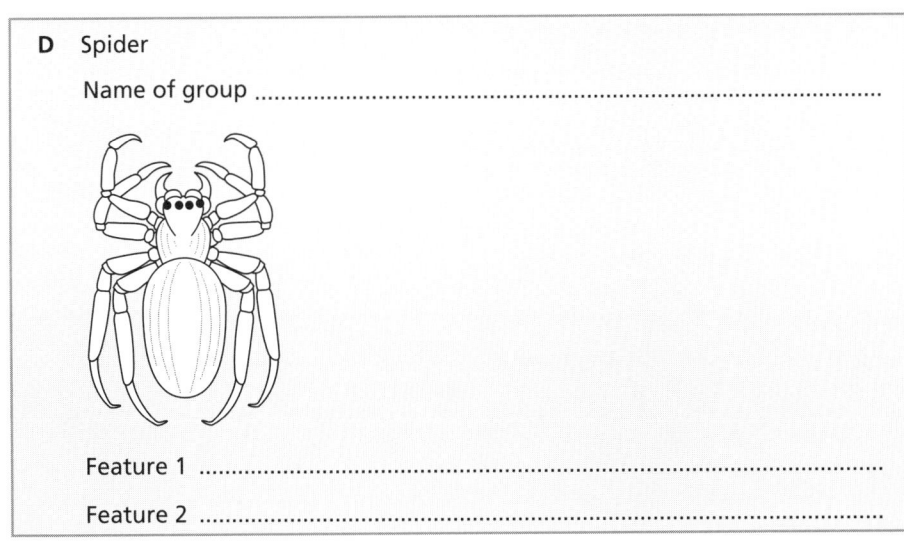

Feature 1 ....

Feature 2 ....

D Spider

Name of group ....

Feature 1 ....

Feature 2 ....

(12 marks)

3 Explain why the dragonfly and spider both belong to the Arthropod group of invertebrates.

....

.... (2 marks)

4 Name **two** features that each of the following pairs of vertebrates have in common and **one** feature that makes them different.

Pair of vertebrates	Common feature	Feature that makes them different
fish and amphibians	1	
	2	
amphibians and reptiles	1	
	2	
birds and mammals	1	
	2	

(9 marks)

5 (a) State **three** features which:

(i) all flowering plants possess

1 ....

2 ....

3 .... (3 marks)

(ii) all flowering plant cells possess.

1 ....

2 ....

3 .... (3 marks)

(b) Complete the table to distinguish between monocotyledons and dicotyledons.

Feature	Monocotyledon	Dicotyledon
leaf shape	long and narrow	
leaf veins		branching
cotyledons	one	
grouping of flower parts, e.g. petals		in fours or fives

(4 marks)

Stretch and challenge

6 (a) Complete the table to give **two** key features of each of the following groups.

	Fungi	Bacteria	Viruses
Features	1	1	1
	2	2	2

(6 marks)

(b) Place the three groups in order of size, starting with the smallest. (1 mark)

1 .... 2 .... 3 ....

(c) Suggest why some scientists have difficulty describing viruses as living organisms.

....

.... (2 marks)

Exam focus

1 The diagram shows four invertebrates.

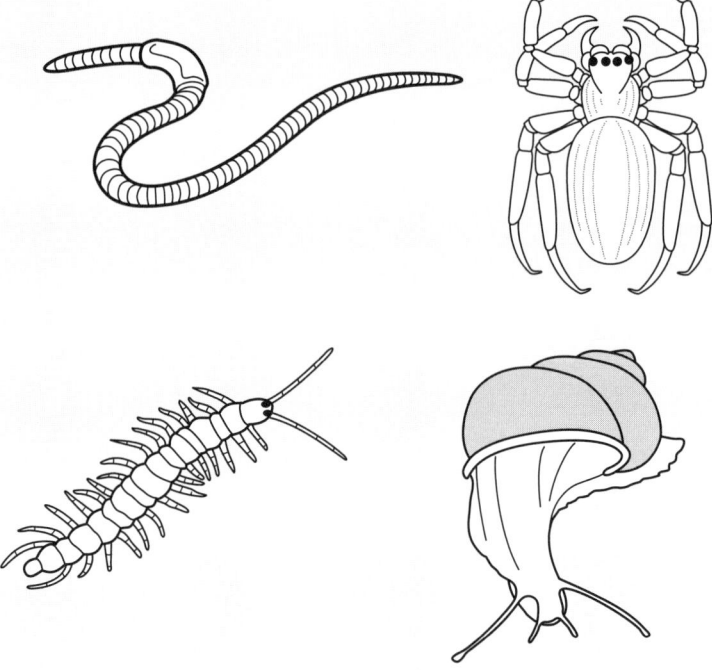

How many of these invertebrates are arthropods? Circle the letter of the correct answer.

A 1
B 2
C 3
D 4

[1]

2   The diagram shows a crab.

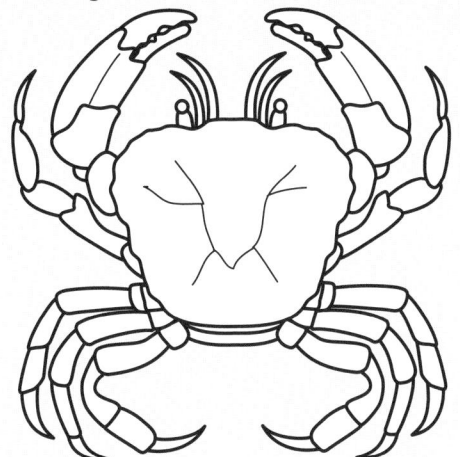

(a) State **two** features, visible in the diagram, which identify the crab as:
   (i) an arthropod

   1 ....

   2 ....[2]

   (ii) a crustacean.

   1 ....

   2 ....[2]

(b) Suggest why a bird that is the same size as the crab uses more energy to survive than the crab does.

   ....

   ....[2]

   [Total: 6 marks]

3 Using simple keys

1 Identify the invertebrate groups labelled **A–G** described on the invertebrate key. Record your answers below.

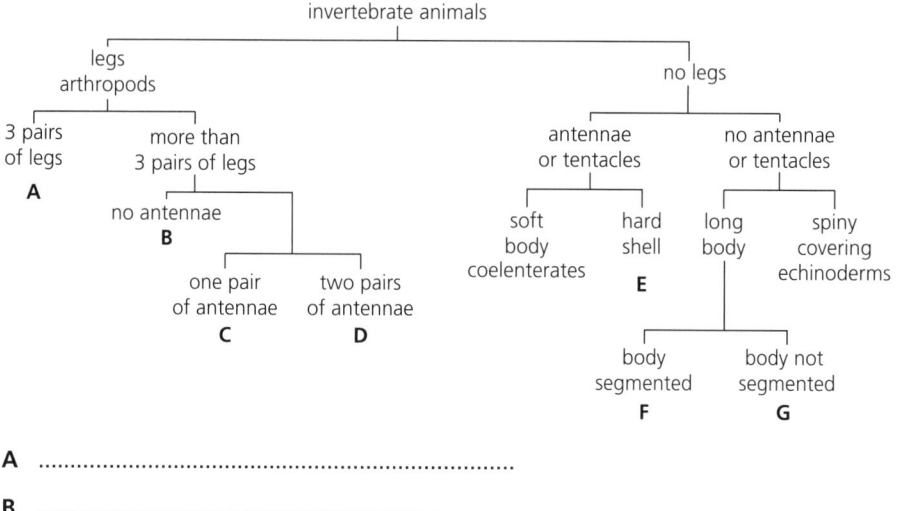

A ....

B ....

C ....

D ....

E ....

F ....

G ....

(7 marks)

2 The diagram shows four species of flowering plants.

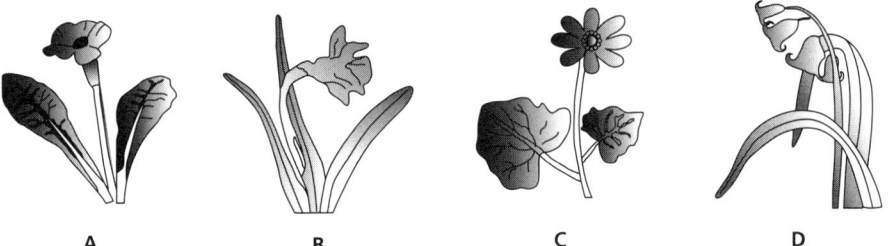

Use the key below to identify the name of each flowering plant. Complete the table by adding the names of the plants and putting a tick in the correct boxes to show how you have identified each plant. Plant **A** has been done for you.

1 a leaves narrow   go to 2

   b leaves broad   go to 3

2 a flowers bell-shaped   *Hyacinthoides non-scripta*

   b flowers trumpet-shaped   *Narcissus pseudonarcissus*

3 a leaves heart-shaped   *Ranunculus ficaria*

   b leaves club-shaped   *Primula vulgaris*

Plant	1a	1b	2a	2b	3a	3b	Name of plant
A	–	✓	–	–	–	✓	*Primula vulgaris*
B							
C							
D							

(3 marks)

Exam focus

1 The diagram shows five species of mollusc.

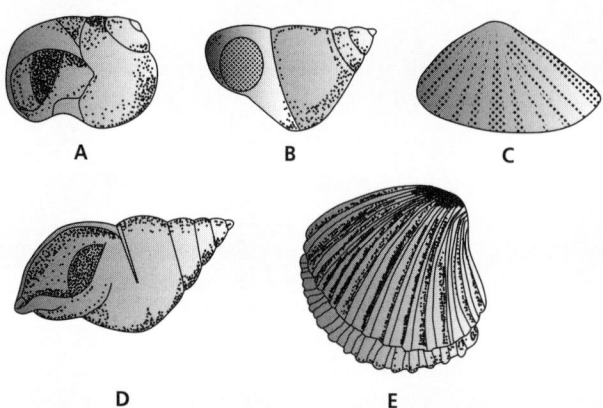

Use the key to identify each species. Write your answers in the table.

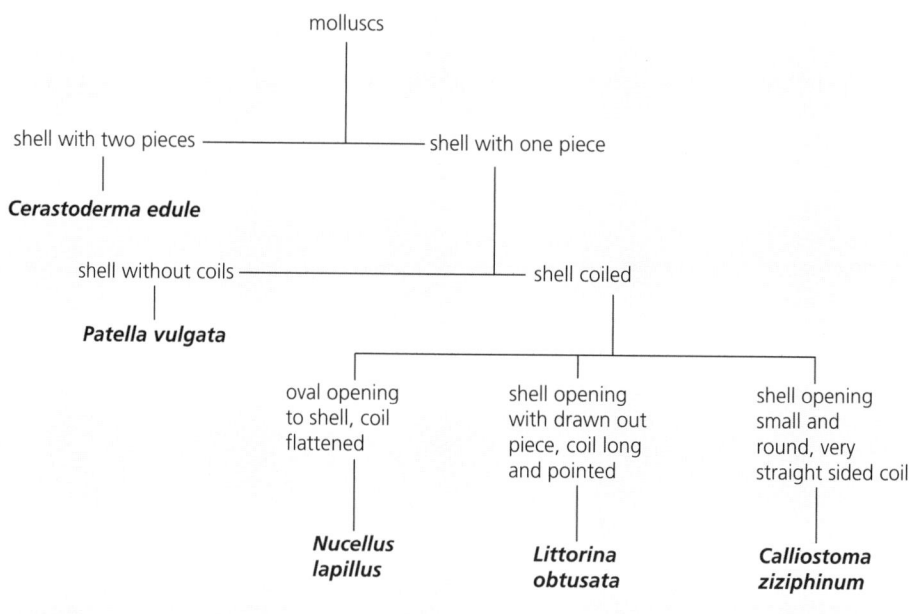

Letter	Species name
A	
B	
C	
D	
E	

[5]

4 Cell structure and organisation

1   State whether each of the statements is true or false. Circle T or F.

(a) The outer layer of an animal cell is a cell wall. T / F

(b) All cells have a nucleus. T / F

(c) Some plant cells have chloroplasts for photosynthesis. T / F

(d) Root cells do not have chloroplasts. T / F

(e) Membranes are strong to stop the cell bursting. T / F

(f) Cell walls are non-living. T / F

(g) Cell walls are freely permeable, allowing water and salts to pass through. T / F

(h) The vacuole of a cell contains organelles such as mitochondria. T / F

(i) DNA is found in the nucleus. T / F

(j) The cytoplasm of some white blood cells can flow to engulf microbes. T / F

(10 marks)

2   (a) Label parts **A–F** on the diagram of the leaf palisade cell.

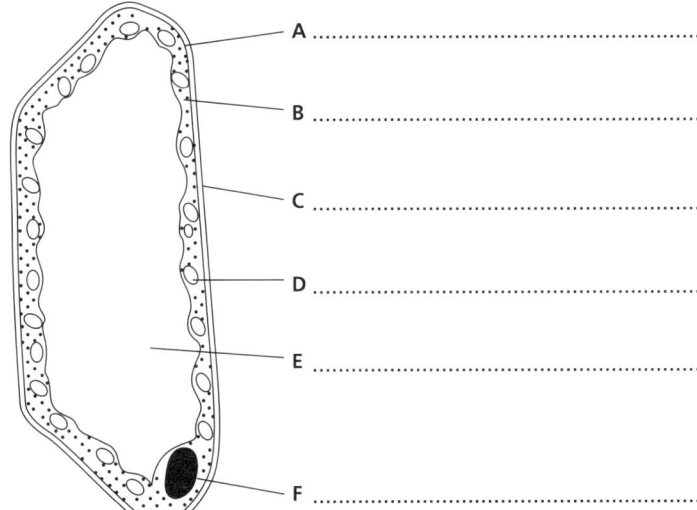

A ....

B ....

C ....

D ....

E ....

F ....

(6 marks)

(b) State **three** parts, present in this cell, which would not be found in an animal cell such as a liver cell.

1 ....

2 ....

3 .... (3 marks)

15

3 Draw lines to match each part of the cell to its description.

Cell part	Description
cell wall	a fluid-filled space surrounded by a membrane
chloroplast	a round or oval structure containing DNA in the form of chromosomes
cytoplasm	a tough, non-living layer made of cellulose; it surrounds the membrane
membrane	jelly-like, with particles and organelles in
nucleus	an organelle containing chlorophyll
sap vacuole	a partially permeable layer that forms a boundary around the cytoplasm

(6 marks)

Stretch and challenge

4 State **two** functions for each of the following cell parts.

(a) Cytoplasm

1 ....

2 ....

(b) Membrane

1 ....

2 ....

(c) Nucleus

1 ....

2 .... (6 marks)

■ *Exam focus*

1 (a) State **three** structural features that are present in both plant cells and animal cells.

1 ....

2 ....

3 .... [3]

(b) (i) Name **one** cell organelle that would be found in a leaf palisade cell but **not** in a root hair cell.

.... [1]

(ii) State the chemical present in this organelle and describe its function.

Chemical ....

Function .... [2]

[Total: 6]

2 (a) Name **two** organelles that distinguish plant cells from animal cells.

1 ....

2 .... [2]

(b) The diagram shows a group of animal cells.

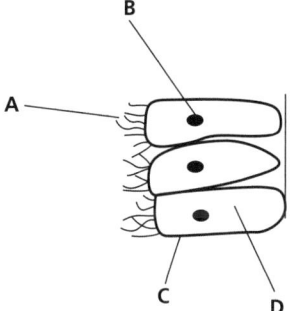

Complete the table by matching each of the functions described to a cell part **A–D**.

Function	Cell part
controls cell activities and development	
contains cell organelles and is the site of chemical reactions	
waft mucus and bacteria away from the lungs	
controls what substances enter and leave the cell	

[4]

[Total: 6]

3 (a) Construct a table to compare the structure of a liver cell with that of a palisade mesophyll cell. [5]

(b) Describe the function of each part of the palisade mesophyll cell.

....
....
....
....
....
.... [6]

[Total: 11]

5 Levels of organisation

1 Put the following terms in order of size from smallest to largest.

| organ | nucleus | chromosome | cell | organ-system | organism | tissue |

☐ ☐ ☐ ☐ ☐ ☐ ☐

(smallest) (largest)

(3 marks)

2 Draw lines to match the terms to the examples. Some of the terms may have links from more than one example.

Example **Term**

- leaf
- heart
- skeleton
- root hair
- spongy mesophyll
- worm

- cell
- organ
- tissue
- organ system
- organism

(6 marks)

3 (a) State the formula for calculating magnification.

(1 mark)

(b) A drawing of a grasshopper measures 12.0 cm from the end of its abdomen to its head, but the actual size of the organism is 2.8 cm. Calculate the magnification of the drawing. Show your working.

(2 marks)

4 When viewed under a microscope at ×100, the apparent size of a nematode is 15 mm. Calculate its actual size. Show your working.

(2 marks)

5 (a) Define the term *tissue*.

....

.... (2 marks)

(b) Complete the table by naming **two** types of animal tissues and **two** types of plant tissues and stating their functions.

Tissue	Name	Function
animal tissue 1		
animal tissue 2		
plant tissue 1		
plant tissue 2		

(8 marks)

Stretch and challenge

6 Name **five** types of cell found in a plant leaf. For each cell, describe its main features and function.

....
....
....
....
....
....
....
....
....
....
....
....
....
....
.... (15 marks)

7 Some cells are specialised by having extensions to them, which have specific functions. Name **one** plant cell and **three** animal cells that are adapted in this way and state their locations and functions.

	Name	Location	Function
plant cell			
animal cell 1			
animal cell 2			
animal cell 3			

(12 marks)

LEVELS OF ORGANISATION

LEVELS OF ORGANISATION

■ *Exam focus*

1 Define the terms *organ*, *organ system* and *tissue*, naming **one** example of each in an animal and in a plant.

....

....

....

....

....

....

....

.... [6]

2 The cells listed in the table below are adapted to their functions by having different numbers of some organelles compared to other cells.

For each cell:

(a) state whether it has more, less or none of the named organelle compared to typical cells [5]

(b) explain how this adaptation benefits the cell's function. [5]

Cell	Organelle(s)	more/less/none	Explanation
muscle cell	mitochondria		
red blood cell	nucleus		
upper epidermal cell	chloroplasts		
liver cell	mitochondria		
xylem	nucleus		

[Total: 10]

3 (a) Explain why a leaf is described as an organ.

....

.... [2]

22

(b) The diagram shows a section through a leaf. Complete the table to identify parts **A–F** and state their main functions.

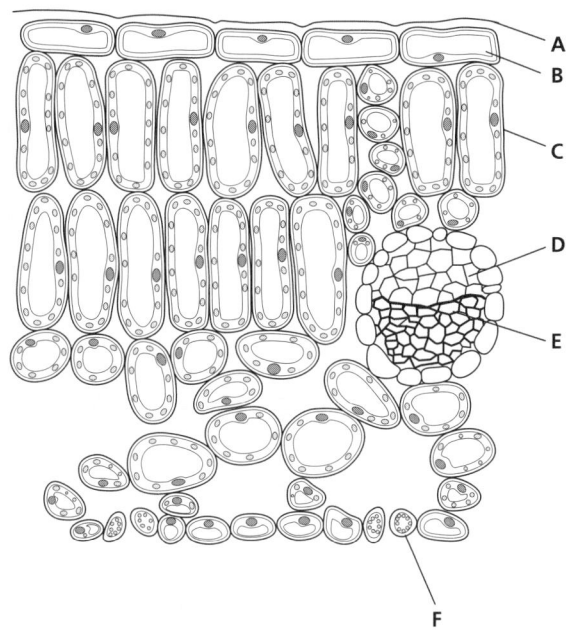

Leaf part	Name	Function
A		
B		
C		
D		
E		
F		

[12]

[Total: 14]

6 Diffusion and active transport

1. Define the term *diffusion*.

   ....

   ....(3 marks)

2. In the lungs a substance diffuses from the alveoli into the blood capillaries.

   (a) (i) Name the substance described. .... (1 mark)

   (ii) State **three** factors that will encourage a fast rate of diffusion for this substance.

   1 ....

   2 ....

   3 ....(3 marks)

   (b) Suggest and explain what would happen to the rate of diffusion, if:

   (i) the temperature in the lungs went down

   ....

   ....(2 marks)

   (ii) the person's breathing rate increased.

   ....

   ....(2 marks)

3. The diagram shows a section through a leaf.

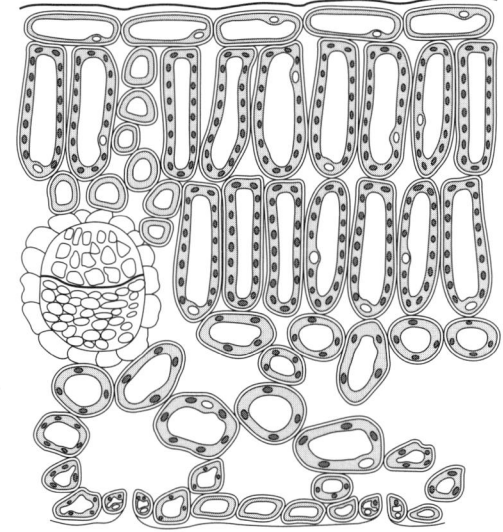

(a) (i) Label the diagram to identify the following parts: air space; palisade mesophyll cell; stoma; upper epidermis. (4 marks)

(ii) On the diagram, draw arrows to show the diffusion of carbon dioxide from the air into the leaf to the palisade mesophyll tissue (for use in photosynthesis). (3 marks)

(b) Suggest why:

(i) diffusion does not tend to occur through the upper epidermis

.... (1 mark)

(ii) the diffusion of carbon dioxide (and therefore the rate of photosynthesis) may slow down on a very hot day.

.... (1 mark)

4 State whether each of the statements is true or false. Circle T or F.

(a) Diffusion can happen in solids, liquids and gases. T / F

(b) Diffusion happens more slowly over longer distances. T / F

(c) Large molecules diffuse faster than small molecules. T / F

(d) In the lungs, carbon dioxide diffuses into the blood and oxygen diffuses out of it. T / F

(e) Animals with a small surface area to volume ratio need a gas exchange organ such as the lungs or gills to make diffusion more efficient. T / F

(f) Diffusion slows down as the concentration gradient decreases. T / F (6 marks)

Stretch and challenge

5 Define the term *active transport*.

....

.... **(3 marks)**

6 Two plants, **A** and **B**, were grown in soil with different nitrate ion concentrations. The concentration of nitrate ions was measured both in the soil and inside the roots of the plants. Both plants were found to be successfully absorbing the nitrate. The table shows the results.

Plant	Concentration of nitrate in the soil / arbitrary units	Concentration of nitrate in the roots / arbitrary units
A	157	156
B	82	114

(a) Complete the table below by stating the process or processes of absorption of nitrate ions in plants **A** and **B**. Give a reason for your choice.

Process(es)	Reason
plant **A**	
plant **B**	

(4 marks)

(b) In another experiment, the roots of plant **B** were treated with cyanide (a respiratory poison). Explain why the movement of nitrates stopped in the plant.

....

.... **(2 marks)**

■ *Exam focus*

1 Which set of statements correctly describes active transport? Circle the letter of the correct set. [1]

	Moves molecules from high concentration to low concentration	Moves molecules from low concentration to high concentration	Energy required	Energy not required
A	✓	✗	✓	✗
B	✗	✓	✗	✓
C	✓	✗	✗	✓
D	✗	✓	✓	✗

2 Cells can obtain substances by diffusion, osmosis and active transport. Complete the table about the absorption of substances into two types of cell.

Type of cell	Substance absorbed	Process(es) used	Gradient: high to low/low to high?	Energy used?
root hair cell	water			
	phosphate	1	1	1
		2	2	2
villus cell in small intestine	glucose	1	1	1
		2	2	2

[15]

3 The diagram shows a section through part of the lungs, associated with gaseous exchange.

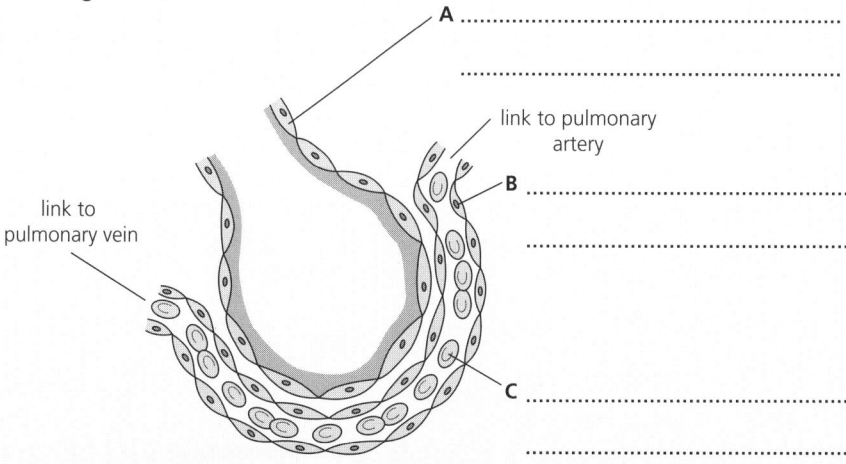

(a) On the diagram, identify parts **A**, **B** and **C**. [3]
(b) On the diagram, draw labelled arrows to show:
   (i) the movement of oxygen [1]
   (ii) the movement of carbon dioxide [1]
   (iii) the direction of blood flow. [1]

(c) (i) By which process is oxygen passed into the blood?

.... [1]

(ii) Explain how a concentration gradient is maintained to move oxygen into the blood.

....

.... [2]

[Total: 9]

4 The diagram shows a section through a villus in the small intestine.

to hepatic portal vein
to lymphatic system

(a) Identify parts **A**, **B** and **C** and state a function for each.

A ....

Function ....

....

B ....

Function ....

....

C ....

Function ....

.... [6]

(b) The cells present in structure **C** have microvilli on their surface. Explain the benefit of these microvilli being present.

....

.... [2]

(c) After a meal, glucose is present in the small intestine in higher concentrations than in the blood.

(i) Name the process by which this glucose would **initially** pass into the bloodstream.

.... [1]

(ii) State **two** ways in which the capillaries in the villus allow the efficient absorption of glucose.

1 ....

2 .... [2]

(d) Active transport is also used for glucose absorption.

(i) Explain when active transport would start to be used for glucose absorption.

.... [1]

(ii) State **one** disadvantage of using active transport to move the glucose.

.... [1]

[Total: 13]

7 Osmosis

1. Complete the paragraph using words from the word list.

active	uptake	dying	flaccid	fully	higher	large	leaves	lower
membrane	osmosis	partially	roots	small	stem	turgid	wall	wilting

   Plants obtain their water through their ………………… using the process of ………………….. The water moves from a region of ………………… concentration to a region of ………………… concentration through the cell …………………. Cells swollen with water are said to be …………………. Cells that have lost a lot of water are ………………….. Temporary loss of water from leaf cells can result in the leaf ………………….. Cell membranes only allow ………………… molecules such as water and minerals to pass through. This means the membrane is ………………… permeable.

   (10 marks)

2. A potato was set up as shown in the diagram. The experiment was left for several hours.

   (a) Predict what would happen to the levels of liquid in the hollow and in the dish. Circle the correct answer.

   Level in the hollow goes up / down.
   Level in the dish goes up / down. **(2 marks)**

   (b) Explain your answers.

   ....
   ....
   ....**(3 marks)**

(c) Suggest why plants die when grown in soil with too much salt.

....
....
.... (3 marks)

Stretch and challenge

3   Place a tick (✓) or a cross (×) in each box to show if each process would be responsible for the movement of the substance into or out of plant cells.

Substance	Diffusion	Osmosis	Active transport
oxygen			
water			
phosphates			
carbon dioxide			

(4 marks)

4   Using terms related to water potential, explain how water moves from the soil into the centre of a root.

....
....
....
....
....
....
.... (4 marks)

5   Six identical potato cores were cut so that they all had the same mass and surface area. Each was placed in a sugar solution of a different concentration and left for 6 hours. They were then reweighed and the percentage change in mass was calculated. The graph shows the results.

Stretch and challenge

Describe and explain the results shown in zones **A**, **B** and **C** of the graph.

Zone **A** ....

....

....

Zone **B** ....

....

....

Zone **C** ....

....

.... (8 marks)

6 (a) State **three** functions of water in a plant.

1 ....

2 ....

3 .... (3 marks)

(b) Describe and explain how water moves:
   (i) from the soil into a plant root

   ....

   ....

   ....

   .... (4 marks)

   (ii) from root epidermal cells to the stem

   ....

   ....

   ....

   .... (4 marks)

   (iii) from a leaf into the air.

   ....

   ....

   ....

   .... (4 marks)

Exam focus

1 (a) Describe and explain what would happen to a plant cell if it was placed in:
   (i) water

   ....

   ....

   .... [4]

   (ii) concentrated sugar solution.

   ....

   ....

   .... [4]

   (b) Drugs such as ecstasy can confuse the brain into thinking the body is dehydrated. The drug user then drinks large amounts of water to satisfy the apparent thirst.
   (i) Describe and explain the potential effects on red blood cells, if the blood plasma became very dilute.

   ....

   ....

   ....

   .... [3]

   (ii) With reference to the function of red blood cells, suggest how this change to the red blood cells could affect the rest of the body.

   ....

   ....

   .... [2]

   [Total: 13]

2 Six potato cores were all cut to the same length and then placed in a range of sugar solutions. After an hour, the cores were removed and remeasured. The results are shown in the table.

Sugar concentration/ mol dm^{-3}	Start length/cm	Length after one hour/cm	Change in length/cm	% change in length
0.0	5.0	5.3		
0.2	5.0	5.1		
0.4	5.0	4.7		
0.6	5.0	4.4		
0.8	5.0	4.3		
1.0	5.0	4.3		

(a) Calculate the change in length of each potato core and write the results in the table. [2]

33

OSMOSIS

The % change in length can be calculated using the equation shown below.

% change in length = $\dfrac{\text{change in length}}{\text{start length}} \times 100$

(b) Calculate the % change in length of each potato core and write the results in the table. [2]

(c) Plot a line graph of % change in length against concentration on the graph paper below. Use concentration as the *x*-axis.

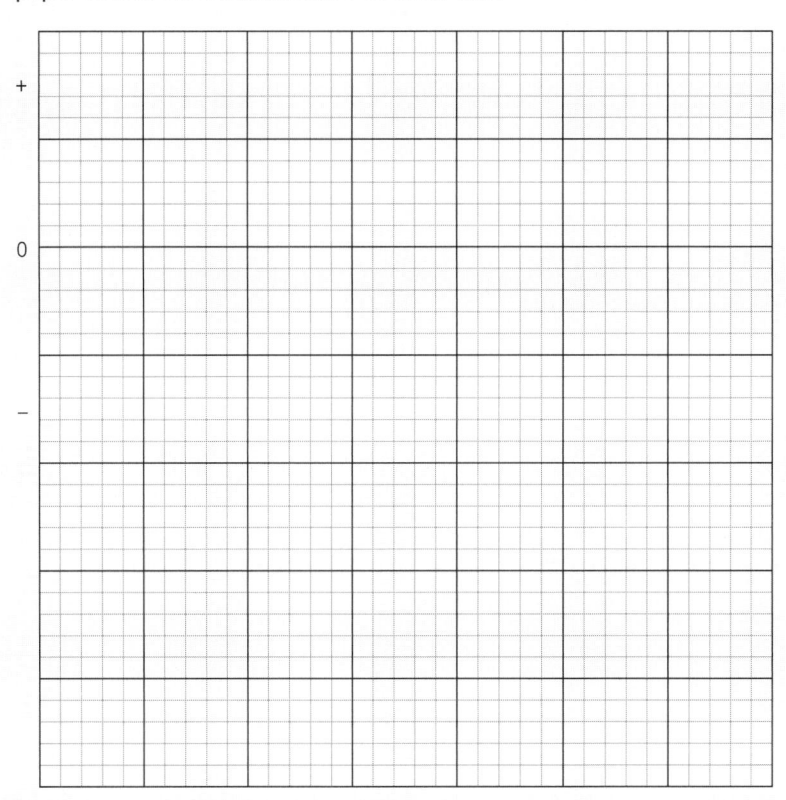

+

0

−

[4]

(d) (i) Use the graph to predict at which sugar concentration there would be no change in length of the potato core.

.... [1]

(ii) Explain why there would be no change in length at this concentration.

....

.... [2]

(e) State **two** ways of making this experiment a fair test.

1 ....

2 .... [2]

(f) Suggest **one** way of making the results more reliable.

.... [1]

[Total: 14]

34

8 Enzymes

1 Define the following terms:
   (a) Catalyst

   ....

   .... (2 marks)

   (b) Enzyme

   ....

   .... (2 marks)

2 The equation shows an enzyme-controlled reaction.

   starch —amylase→ maltose

   (a) Fill in the boxes to annotate the equation with the following terms:

   | enzyme   end product   substrate | (3 marks)

   (b) State **two** differences between a molecule such as starch (at the start of digestion) and glucose (an end product of digestion).

   1 ....

   2 .... (2 marks)

   (c) Explain why a different enzyme such as protease would not control the same reaction as amylase.

   ....

   ....

   .... (2 marks)

35

3 (a) The graph shows the effect of temperature on the rate of an enzyme-controlled reaction.

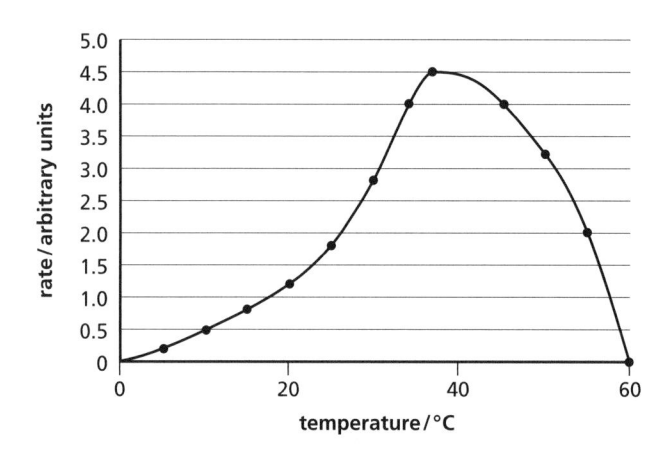

[Graph: rate/arbitrary units vs temperature/°C, showing a curve peaking at about 35°C at rate 4.5, declining to 0 at 60°C]

On the graph, use label lines to add the following labels:

denaturing is taking place here
optimum reaction rate
the reaction is slow here
the reaction is speeding up fastest here (4 marks)

(b) Predict and explain what would happen if:
  (i) the reaction mixture at 10 °C was warmed up to 30 °C

  ....
  ....
  ....(2 marks)

  (ii) the reaction mixture at 60 °C was cooled down to 30 °C.

  ....
  ....(2 marks)

4 State **three** factors that affect the rate of enzyme-controlled reactions.

1 ....
2 ....
3 ....(3 marks)

Stretch and challenge

5 Name **two** industries that use enzymes in making foods and describe the role of enzymes in these processes.

Industry 1 ....

Description ....

....

Industry 2 ....

Description ....

.... (6 marks)

6 (a) The diagram shows a fermenter, used to manufacture enzymes.

Describe the role of each of the following parts:
(i) Paddles

....

.... (1 mark)

(ii) Filter

....

.... (1 mark)

(iii) Feedstock

....

.... (1 mark)

(b) What types of organisms are used to manufacture enzymes?

.... (2 marks)

(c) Describe how intracellular enzymes are extracted from microorganisms.

....

.... (2 marks)

■ Exam focus

1 Enzymes are used in biological washing powders to remove fat and protein stains.

  (a) State which enzyme would be used to remove:

  (i) fat stains .... [1]

  (ii) protein stains. .... [1]

  (b) Explain why enzyme-based washing powers are more efficient than ordinary washing powders.

  ....

  .... [2]

  (c) Non-enzyme based washing powders work best at high temperatures. Explain why biological washing powders are **not** used at high temperatures.

  ....

  .... [2]

  (d) When protein stains such as blood are digested, amino acids are produced. Explain why these are easier to remove than the undigested blood stain.

  ....

  .... [2]

  [Total: 8]

2 Enzymes are involved in the process of seed germination. Food stored in seeds is often in the form of starch.

  (a) (i) Name the enzyme needed to digest starch. .... [1]

  (ii) Name the product of this digestion. .... [1]

  (iii) Suggest **two** uses of this product in the germinating seed.

   1 ....

   2 .... [2]

  (iv) State **two** physical differences between starch and the product of its digestion.

   1 ....

   2 .... [2]

  The process of germination cannot start until the seed has taken in water, but the testa of the seed is impermeable.

  (b) (i) State how water enters the seed to trigger germination.

   .... [1]

  (ii) Suggest **two** reasons why water is needed for germination.

   1 ....

   2 .... [2]

  [Total: 9]

9 Nutrition and nutrients

1 On the diagrams of food molecules:
   (i) name each of the nutrients shown (3 marks)
   (ii) state one use of the nutrient in the body (3 marks)
   (iii) add labels to the diagrams, using words from the list below. You can use the words once, or more than once. (7 marks)

   | amino acid   fatty acid   chemical bond   glucose unit   glycerol |

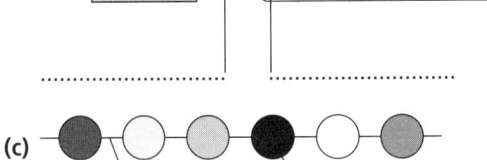

   (a) .... 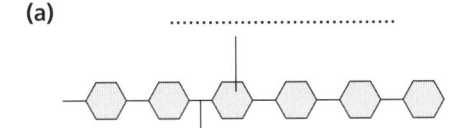
       (i) ....
       (ii) ....
           ....

   (b) .... 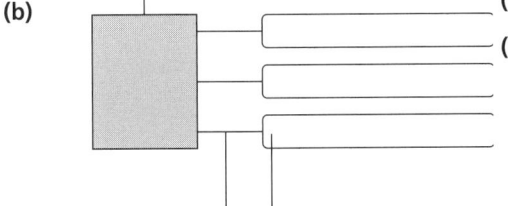
       (i) ....
       (ii) ....
           ....
           ....

   (c) .... 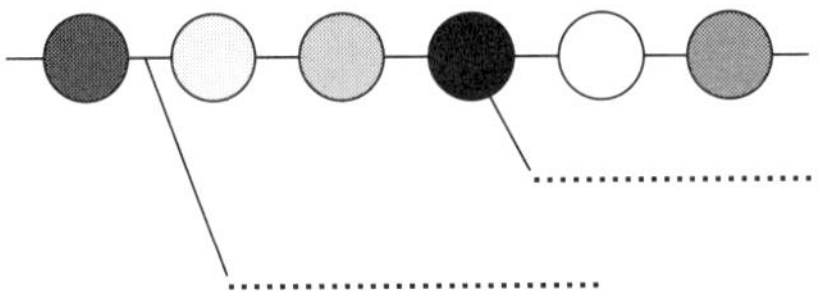
       (i) ....
       (ii) ....
           ....
           ....

2 Draw lines to match the statements to the food tests and the results.

Food tested	Chemical reagent used	Colour for a positive result
reducing sugar	iodine solution	blue-black
fat	Benedict's solution	violet (halo)
protein	ethanol	brick red
starch	Biuret solution (sodium hydroxide + copper sulfate solution)	white emulsion

   (4 marks)

3 Name the nutrient that is responsible for each of the following symptoms, when in short supply.

(a) Anaemia – constant tiredness, lack of energy ....

(b) Dehydration ....

(c) Rickets and slow blood clotting ....

(d) Constipation ....

(e) Scurvy .... (5 marks)

Stretch and challenge

4 Describe how microorganisms are used in the following food industries:
(a) Baking

....

....

.... (3 marks)

(b) Yoghurt-making

....

....

.... (3 marks)

5 Complete the following table with the details for three groups of food additives.

Name of group	Function of additive	Advantage	Disadvantage

(12 marks)

■ *Exam focus*

1. A shortage of which food nutrient can result in the deficiency disease scurvy? Circle the letter of the correct answer.

   A vitamin C
   B vitamin D
   C iron
   D calcium [1]

2. What sub-units are found in proteins? Circle the letter of the correct answer.

   A fatty acids
   B amino acids
   C glucose
   D lactic acid [1]

3. Beef sausages and Quorn sausages are both good sources of protein. The nutritional content of these food products is shown in the table.

food product	Nutritional content/100 g of product					
	energy/kJ	protein/g	saturated fat/g	fibre/g	iron/mg	calcium/mg
beef sausage	1395	17.9	10.7	0.0	1.57	11.0
Quorn sausage	691	14.0	0.6	55	0.5	42.5

   (a) Using the data from the table, state and explain **two** reasons why Quorn sausage may be healthier than beef sausage as a major item in the diet.

   1 ....

   ....

   2 ....

   .... [4]

   (b) Beef sausage contains more iron than Quorn sausage.
   (i) Suggest an additional source of iron for a person eating Quorn sausage in their diet.

   .... [1]

   (ii) State the function of iron in the body.

   .... [2]

   (iii) Outline the effects of a deficiency of iron.

   .... [2]

   ....

(c) Quorn sausage contains a mycoprotein.

  (i) State what mycoprotein is made of..

  .... [1]

  (ii) Suggest **two** reasons why mycoprotein is preferable to other single-cell protein foods.

  1 ....

  2 .... [2]

(d) The food chain involved in the production of mycoprotein is much shorter than that used to produce beef. Explain why it is an advantage to the top consumer to obtain food from a short food chain.

....

.... [2]

[Total: 14]

10 Plant nutrition

1 (a) Write the **word equation** for photosynthesis. (2 marks)

   (b) Name the molecule that glucose is converted to:
      (i) for transport around the plant ....
      (ii) for storage. ....(2 marks)
   (c) Explain why chlorophyll is important in the process of photosynthesis.
      .... (1 mark)
   (d) Suggest **three** negative impacts to animal life on the Earth if plants were destroyed on a large scale.
      1 ....
      2 ....
      3 .... (3 marks)

2 With reference to a leaf, name the cells that:
   (a) carry out most photosynthesis ....(1 mark)
   (b) control the exchange of gases such as carbon dioxide, oxygen and
       water vapour ....(1 mark)
   (c) secrete a waxy cuticle for protection and waterproofing
       .... (1 mark)
   (d) transfer water into the leaf from the roots and stem ....(1 mark)
   (e) carry away the products of photosynthesis. ....(1 mark)

3 Explain why plants fail to grow well when there is a deficiency of:
   (a) nitrate ions
       ....
       .... (2 marks)
   (b) magnesium ions.
       ....
       .... (2 marks)

4 The following statements relate to the effects of applying too much nitrogen fertiliser, but they are in the wrong order. Place them in the correct sequence in the blank boxes. **(2 marks)**

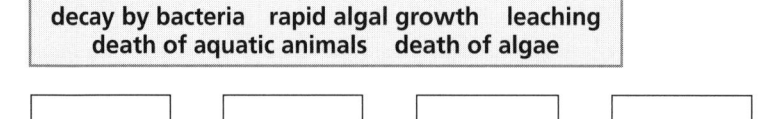

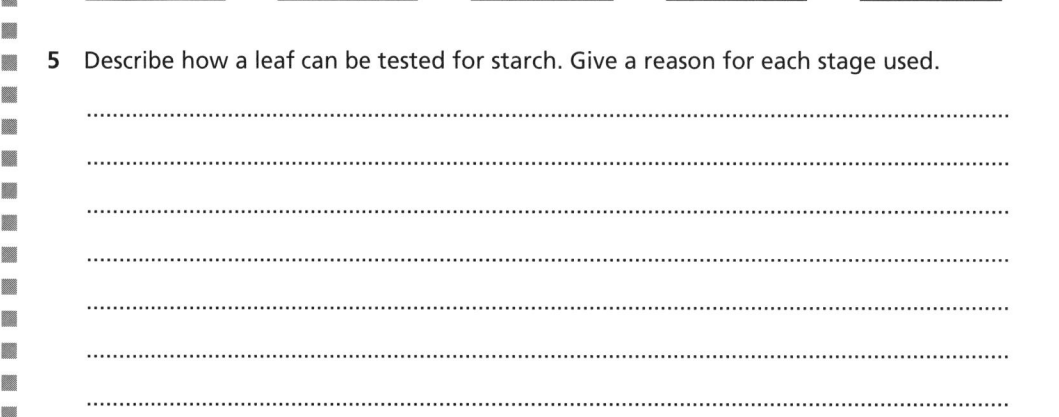

| decay by bacteria   rapid algal growth   leaching |
| death of aquatic animals   death of algae |

☐ → ☐ → ☐ → ☐ → ☐

5 Describe how a leaf can be tested for starch. Give a reason for each stage used.

....

....

....

....

....

....

.... **(5 marks)**

Stretch and challenge

6 (a) The diagram shows the amount of light of different colours absorbed by chlorophyll.

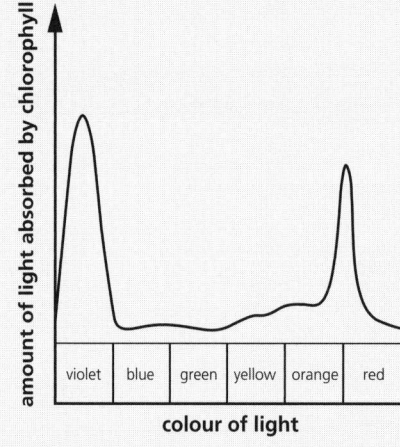

(graph: y-axis "amount of light absorbed by chlorophyll"; x-axis "colour of light" with categories violet, blue, green, yellow, orange, red; large peak over violet/blue, smaller peak over orange/red)

Stretch and challenge

State which colours would be:

(i) most useful to the plant .... (2 marks)

(ii) least useful to the plant. .... (1 mark)

(b) Some pond plants such as *Elodea* produce bubbles of oxygen when exposed to light. Describe how you could carry out an experiment to study the effect of light intensity on photosynthesis in *Elodea*. Make sure you state how you would make the investigation a fair test.

....

....

....

....

....

....

....

....

....

....

....

....

....

....

....

....

....

.... (6 marks)

■ *Exam focus*

1. Which type of leaf cell has the most chloroplasts? Circle the letter of the correct answer.
   A upper epidermis
   B palisade mesophyll
   C spongy mesophyll
   D guard cell [1]

2. (a) Waterlogged soil is often low in nitrogen ions.
   (i) Describe what the plants grown in this sort of soil would look like and explain why they would not grow well.

   ....

   ....

   .... [3]

   (ii) Suggest what a farmer could do to improve the growth of these plants.

   ....

   .... [2]

   (b) Outline the effects of a deficiency of magnesium ions on plants.

   ....

   ....

   .... [3]

   [Total: 8]

3. In Europe, plants in a greenhouse can grow bigger and faster than those grown outside, because of the removal of limiting factors.
   (a) Define the term *limiting factor*.

   ....

   .... [2]

   (b) State **two** conditions, affecting the rate of photosynthesis, that are improved in a greenhouse and explain how each affects plant growth.

   Condition 1 ....

   Explanation ....

   ....

   ....

   Condition 2 ....

   Explanation ....

   ....

   .... [6]

   [Total: 8]

4 Outline an experiment which could be carried out to show that plants need carbon dioxide for photosynthesis.

....

....

....

....

....

....

....

.... [8]

5 The diagram shows cells found in a plant leaf.

A ....

B ....

C ....

D ....

(a) (i) On the diagram, name each of the cells. [4]

(ii) Write the letters of the cells in the boxes below, in the order in which light would pass through them in a leaf. [2]

(b) Vascular bundles are also found in leaves. State **two** types of cell found in vascular bundles and outline their functions.

Cell type 1 ....

Function ....

Cell type 2 ....

Function .... [6]

[Total: 12]

11 Human diet

1 A teenager ate the same main meal each day: a hamburger in a white bread bun, with chips and a glass of cola. The table shows the nutritional value of the food eaten.

Food	Quantity /g	Energy /kJ	Protein /g	Animal fat/g	Carbohydrate /g	Calcium /mg	Iron /mg	Vitamin C/mg
burger	150	1560	30	15	30	50	4	0
bread	90	950	7	2	50	90	1	0
chips	200	2100	8	20	70	25	2	20
cola	300	550	0	0	30	0	0	0

(a) With reference to the nutritional data, state **two** nutritional advantages and **two** disadvantages of eating this meal. Explain your answers.

Advantage 1 ....

Explanation ....

Advantage 2 ....

Explanation ....

Disadvantage 1 ....

Explanation ....

Disadvantage 2 ....

Explanation .... (4 marks)

(b) Suggest **two** long-term effects of continuing to eat this meal regularly.

1 ....

2 .... (2 marks)

(c) This diet could be described as unbalanced.
  (i) Define the term *balanced diet*.

  ....

  .... (2 marks)

  (ii) State **one** food group missing from the diet in the table.

  .... (1 mark)

2 State **three** causes of malnutrition.

1 ....

2 ....

3 .... (3 marks)

3 (a) State **two** long-term effects on a man of drinking excess alcohol.

1 ....

2 .... **(2 marks)**

(b) Explain why a woman should not drink alcohol during pregnancy.

....

.... **(2 marks)**

Stretch and challenge

4 There are a number of problems with food availability around the world. Food shortages can lead to famine.

(a) State and describe **three** other problems that can lead to famine.

....

....

....

....

....

.... **(6 marks)**

(b) Fresh food can rot quickly. Outline **two** ways of increasing the storage life of food.

1 ....

2 .... **(2 marks)**

HUMAN DIET

49

■ *Exam focus*

1 Complete the table by:
  (i) naming **five** components of a balanced diet, other than vitamins and minerals [5]
  (ii) stating the function of the component [5]
  (iii) stating **one** good food source. [5]

	Component	Function	Good food source
1			
2			
3			
4			
5			

[Total: 15]

2 Scurvy and rickets are two deficiency diseases. Complete the table by:
  (i) stating the constituent that is lacking in the diet to cause the disease [2]
  (ii) describing the symptoms of the disease [2]
  (iii) naming a food that could prevent the disease. [2]

Deficiency disease	Constituent	Symptoms	Food
scurvy			
rickets			

[Total: 6]

12 Digestion and absorption

1 On the diagram of the alimentary canal, add labels to name parts **A–H**.

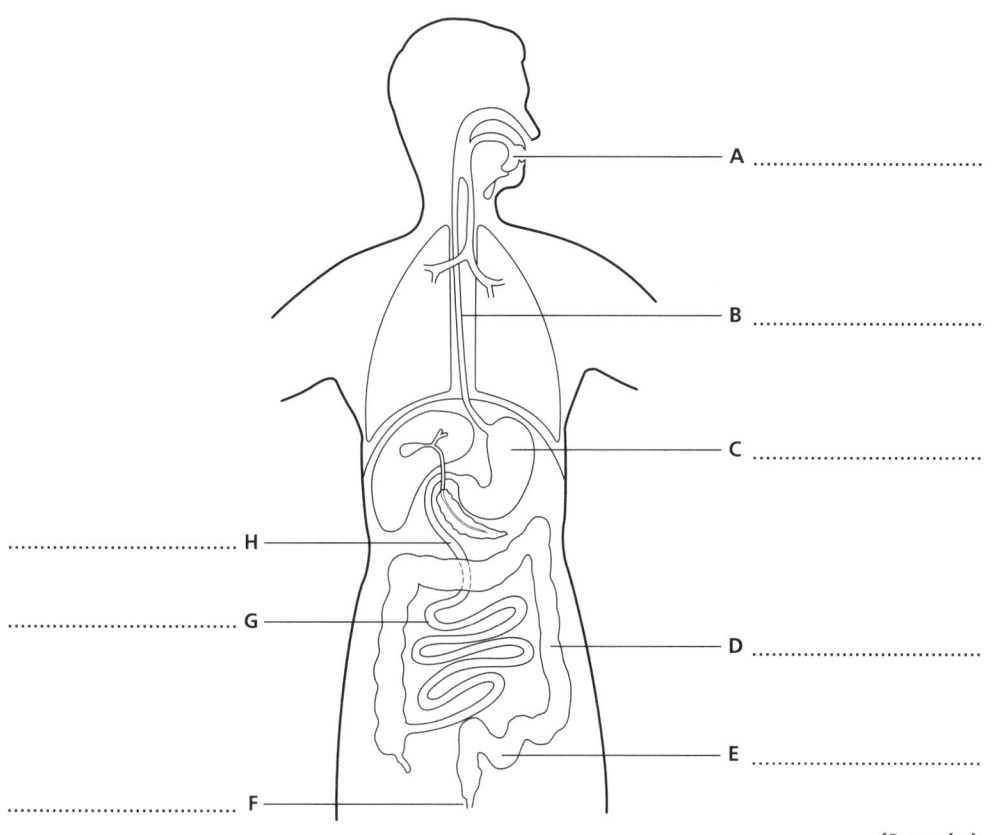

A ....

B ....

C ....

H ....

G ....

D ....

E ....

F ....

(8 marks)

2 (a) Draw lines to match each of the organs to its function. One has been done for you.

(7 marks)

Organ	Function
anus	food is ingested here
colon	a tube, carrying boluses of food between mouth and stomach
duodenum	has an acid pH and proteins are digested here
ileum	first part of the small intestine
mouth	absorption of the products of digestion takes place here
oesophagus (gullet)	muscular, to control the egestion of faeces
rectum	absorption of water
stomach	stores faeces

(The line drawn matches "mouth" to "food is ingested here".)

(b) List the digestive organs from part (a) in the correct sequence in the boxes below.

mouth → ☐ → ☐ → ☐ → ☐ → ☐ → ☐ → ☐

(2 marks)

3 Complete the table to compare the types of human tooth. (6 marks)

Name	incisor		premolar	
Description		slightly more pointed than incisors		four / five cusps two / three roots
Function	biting off pieces of food		tearing and grinding food	

4 (a) Distinguish between physical and chemical digestion.

....

....

....

....

....

....

....

.... **(4 marks)**

(b) Describe the digestion of starch and protein. Include details of the organs, enzymes involved, the conditions they need and the end products.

....

....

....

....

....

....

....

....

.... **(8 marks)**

Stretch and challenge

5 Outline the arguments for and against adding fluoride to public water supplies.

....

....

....

....

....

....

.... **(4 marks)**

Exam focus

1 Which statement correctly identifies the cause of tooth decay? Circle the letter of the correct statement.

   A Sugar attacks the tooth enamel.
   B Alkalis attack the tooth enamel.
   C Bacteria produce acid, which attacks the tooth enamel.
   D Food containing bacteria attacks the tooth enamel. [1]

2 (a) The diagram shows a section through a human tooth.

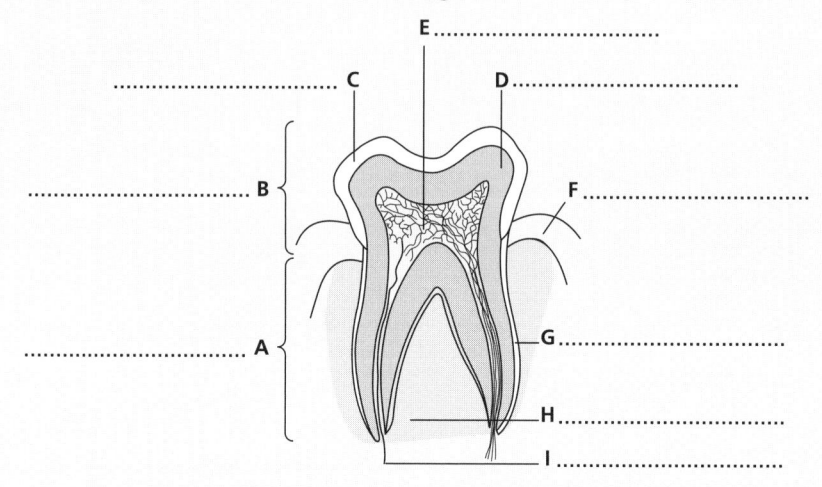

   (i) State the type of tooth shown and explain your answer.

     Type of tooth ....

     Explanation .... [2]

   (ii) On the diagram, label parts **A–J**. [9]

(b) (i) Which layer of the tooth is the hardest? .... [1]

   (ii) Name **one** vitamin and **one** mineral needed to develop this layer.

     Vitamin ....

     Mineral .... [2]

   (iii) Name **one** mineral sometimes added to water or toothpaste to resist tooth

     decay. .... [1]

(c) Outline the process of tooth decay.

   ....

   ....

   ....

   .... [6]

[Total: 21]

3 The diagram shows a section through a villus in the small intestine.

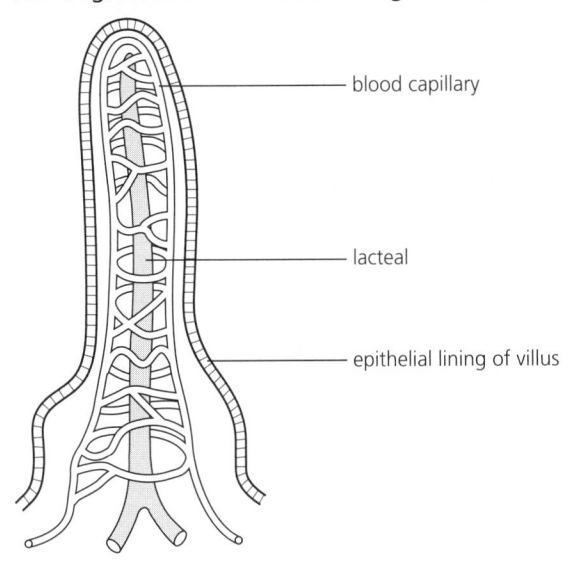

- blood capillary
- lacteal
- epithelial lining of villus

(a) Explain why most food molecules need to be digested before being absorbed.

....

....[2]

(b) Name the processes involved in the absorption of digested food.

....[2]

(c) Describe and explain how the epithelial lining is adapted to absorb digested foods efficiently.

....

....

....[3]

(d) Outline the roles of the following parts in a villus.

　1 Blood capillaries

　　...

　　...

　2 Lacteal

　　...

　　..[4]

[Total: 11]

4 The diagram shows a side view of a human abdomen.

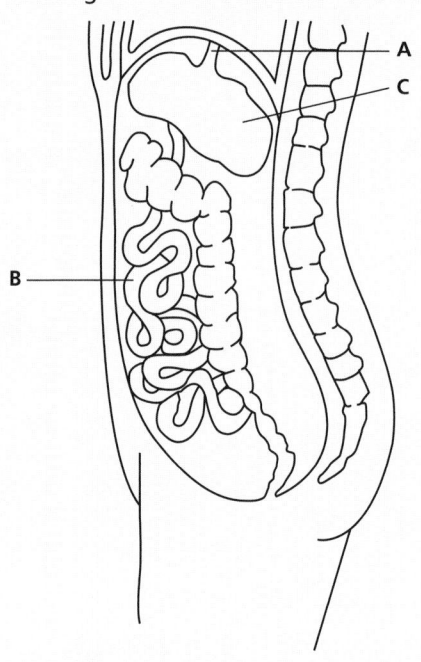

(a) Complete the table by identifying parts **A** and **B**. For each part, state **one** function and **one** structural feature which adapts it to its function.

Part	Name	Function	Structural feature
A			
B			

[6]

(b) (i) State the type of food digested in organ **C**. ....[1]

(ii) Outline how organ **C** achieves the digestion of this food.

....

....

....[3]

(iii) Outline what happens in the liver to the end product of digestion of this food.

....

....

....[4]

[Total: 14]

13 Transport in plants

1 Distinguish between the terms *transpiration* and *translocation*.

   ....
   ....
   ....
   .... (4 marks)

2 (a) State **three** functions of plant roots.

   1 ....
   2 ....
   3 .... (3 marks)

   (b) Describe how root hair cells are adapted for their function.

   ....
   ....(2 marks)

   (c) The diagram shows a section through a root.

   List the parts through which water passes to get to the plant stem, putting them in the correct order. (Clue: only four parts are involved.)

   .... (4 marks)

3 (a) State **three** factors that lead to an increase in the rate of transpiration.

   1 ....
   2 ....
   3 .... (3 marks)

   (b) Outline how wilting can occur in a young plant.

   ....
   ....
   ....
   .... (3 marks)

Stretch and challenge

4 (a) State the term used for plants that are modified to survive in conditions where there is a lack of water.

.... (1 mark)

(b) Name **one** plant that survives in very dry conditions and describe its modifications.

Name ....

Modifications ....

....

....

....

.... (3 marks)

(c) Explain how systemic pesticides can be used to protect a plant crop.

....

....

.... (3 marks)

■ *Exam focus*

1 What is the correct order of tissues through which water passes from soil to a leaf? Circle the letter of the correct answer.

   A root hairs → endodermis → cortex → xylem
   B endodermis → root hairs → cortex → xylem
   C root hairs → cortex → endodermis → xylem
   D cortex → endodermis → root hairs → xylem [1]

2 The diagram shows an aphid feeding from phloem tubes in a plant stem.

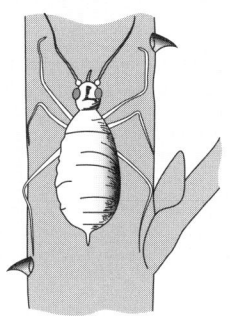

   What type of food would the aphid **not** receive? Circle the letter of the correct answer.

   A sucrose
   B amino acids
   C water
   D mineral salts [1]

3 A number of processes are involved in the movement of substances into and around a plant. Complete the table by defining each term and explaining how it is important to a plant.

Process	Definition	Explanation
diffusion		
osmosis		
active transport		
transpiration		

[12]

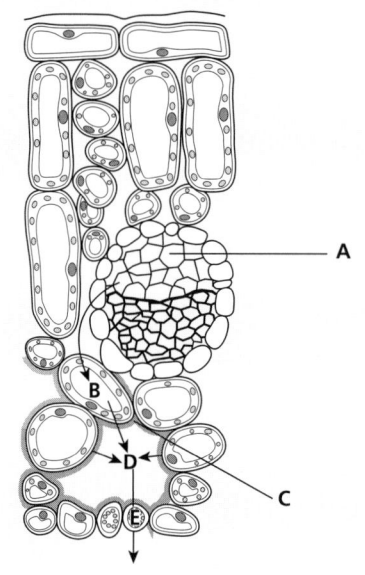

4 (a) The diagram shows a section through part of a leaf.

With reference to the features labelled **A–E**, outline the process of water loss from the leaf.

....

....

....

....

....

....

....

.... [6]

(b) Explain how wilting occurs.

....

....

....

....

....

.... [4]

[Total: 10]

14 Transport in humans

1 **(a)** State which heart chambers contain oxygenated blood.

.... (2 marks)

(b) Name **three** different blood vessels, directly associated with the heart, which carry oxygenated blood.

....

.... (3 marks)

2 **(a)** Define the term *tissue*.

....

.... (2 marks)

(b) What type of tissue is the left ventricle made of?

.... (1 mark)

(c) State **one** property of this tissue.

.... (1 mark)

(d) Explain why the left ventricle has a thicker wall than the right ventricle.

....

....

.... (3 marks)

3 Imagine you are a red blood cell returning to the heart from the renal vein. Describe your journey to the lungs, naming all the main blood vessels and structures you pass through on the way. Also explain how each of these structures enables your movement.

....

....

....

....

....

....

....

....

....

.... (10 marks)

4   The table shows the pulse rate of an athlete before, during and after exercise.

Time/min	0.0	1.0	1.5	2.0	2.5	3.0	3.5	4.0	4.5	5.0	5.5	6.0	6.5	7.0	7.5	8.0	8.5	9.0	9.5	10.0
Pulse rate /beats per min	60	60	68	84	100	120	124	128	124	112	100	92	86	74	68	60	56	60	60	60

(a) Plot the data on the graph paper below, using time as the *x*-axis and pulse rate as the *y*-axis.

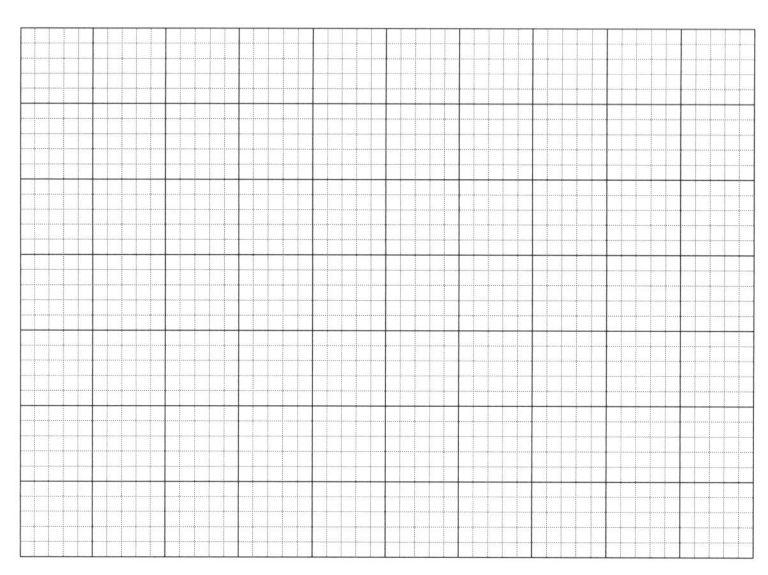

(4 marks)

(b) (i) State the athlete's resting pulse rate.

.... (1 mark)

(ii) Suggest when the exercise started.

.... (1 mark)

(iii) At what time did the pulse rate first return to the resting pulse rate?

.... (1 mark)

(iv) Explain why the pulse rate increased during exercise.

....

....

.... (3 marks)

(v) On the graph, sketch a line to represent the pulse rate of a less fit person doing the same exercise. (3 marks)

(vi) Explain why regular exercise is important in maintaining a healthy heart.

....

.... **(2 marks)**

(c) Complete the table about four main causes of heart attack and preventative measures. The first has been done for you.

Cause of heart attack	Preventative measure
1 lack of exercise	start taking regular exercise
2	
3	
4	

5 Draw a section through an artery. On your drawing, label the main features and add annotations to distinguish this blood vessel from a vein.

(5 marks)

TRANSPORT IN HUMANS

6 The diagram below shows the double circulatory system.

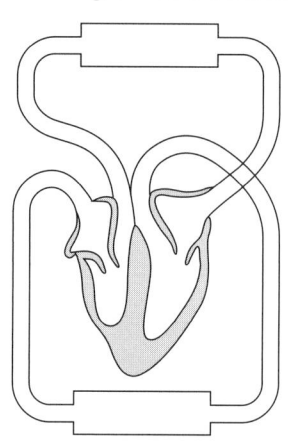

On the diagram:
- **(a)** label the two boxes (2 marks)
- **(b)** add arrows to the blood vessels and heart chambers to show the flow of blood (2 marks)
- **(c)** shade the heart chambers and blood vessels that carry deoxygenated blood. (4 marks)

7 Complete the crossword puzzle about blood cells, using the clues below.

Across
3 the liquid part of the blood (6)
4 produces antibodies to fight disease (10)
5 responsible for blood clotting (8)

Down
1 combines with oxygen in red blood cells (11)
2 present in white blood cells, but not in red blood cells (7)

(5 marks)

Stretch and challenge

8 Explain briefly how the structure of a capillary is related to its function.

....
....
....
....
.... (3 marks)

9 Outline the role of the immune system in:
   (a) antibody production

....
....
....
....
.... (5 marks)

   (b) phagocytosis.

....
....
.... (3 marks)

10 State briefly how tissue rejection can be prevented after an organ transplant.

....
....
.... (3 marks)

11 State **three** functions of the lymphatic system.

....
....
....
.... (3 marks)

■ Exam focus

1 Which statement describes the structure and function of a lymphocyte? Circle the letter of the correct answer.

	Structure	Function
A	has no nucleus	transport of oxygen
B	has a nucleus	engulfs bacteria
C	has a nucleus	produces antibodies
D	has no nucleus	transport of water

[1]

2 The diagram shows a section through the heart.

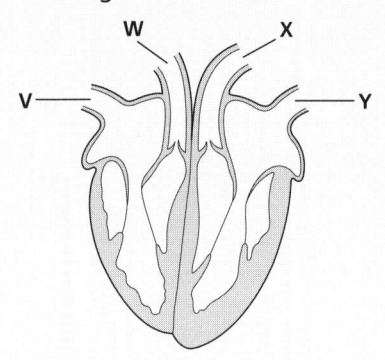

Which two blood vessels carry blood away from the heart? Circle the letter of the correct answer.

A V and Y
B W and X
C V and X
D W and Y

[1]

3 (a) Identify the parts of the heart labelled **A–M** on the diagram below.

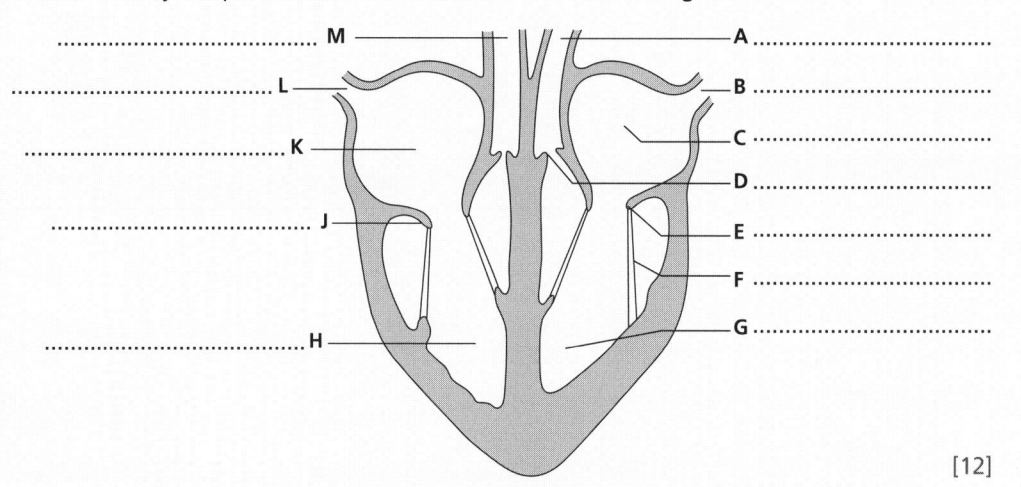

[12]

(b) Name each of the parts of the heart described below.
    (i) the chamber that receives deoxygenated blood from a vein

....

(ii) the blood vessel that passes blood from the lungs to the heart

....

(iii) the valve found in the pulmonary artery ....

(iv) the heart chamber with the thickest wall ....

(v) the tissues that stop heart valves from turning inside out ....

(vi) the main vein of the body ....

(vii) the blood vessel that passes blood from the heart to the main body organs

....

(viii) the valve responsible for preventing the backflow of blood into the right

atrium. .... [8]

[Total: 20]

4 (a) Define the term *double circulation*.

....

.... [2]

(b) Complete the table by describing **two** distinguishing features of arteries, veins and capillaries. [6]

Blood vessel	Distinguishing features
artery	1
	2
vein	1
	2
capillary	1
	2

[Total: 8]

5 (a) State **one** function for each of the following components of the blood.

(i) plasma ....

(ii) red blood cell ....

(iii) lymphocyte ....

(iv) phagocyte ....

(v) platelet .... [5]

(b) State **one** observable feature for each of the blood cells listed below.

(i) red blood cell ....

(ii) lymphocyte ....

(iii) phagocyte .... [3]

[Total: 8]

15 Respiration

1 (a) Write the **word equation** for aerobic respiration.

.... (2 marks)

(b) State the form in which the energy produced is stored in muscles.

....(1 mark)

(c) (i) Name the waste product of anaerobic respiration in muscles.

....(1 mark)

(ii) Explain why a build-up of this waste product is a problem for an athlete.

....

.... (2 marks)

2 When yeast respires anaerobically, two products are produced. Name the products and identify a food manufacturing process that makes use of each product.

Product	Food manufacturing process
1	
2	

(4 marks)

3 (a) Starting with the mouth, list the structures which air passes through in order for oxygen to be absorbed by a red blood cell.

mouth → ☐ → ☐ → ☐ → ☐ → red blood cell

(4 marks)

(b) (i) Name the process by which oxygen passes across the wall of the alveolus into the bloodstream.

....(1 mark)

(ii) List **four** features of a gaseous exchange surface that make it efficient.

1 ....

2 ....

3 ....

4 .... (4 marks)

4 Define the following terms:

(a) *Tidal volume*..

.... (2 marks)

(b) *Vital capacity.* ....
....(2 marks)

5 The following anagrams are all terms associated with smoking cigarettes. Rearrange the letters to identify the terms. Use the clues to help you.

Anagram	Clue	Answer
crance	disease caused by smoking	
emmahypes	disease caused by smoking	
gluns	organ of the body	
accengiorn	cancer-causing chemical	
oncrab exmoonid	gas in cigarette smoke	
rat	chemical in cigarette smoke	
stonchibri	disease caused by smoking	
teniconi	chemical in cigarette smoke	
toccbao	leaf used for smoking	
trefil	part of a cigarette designed to remove tar	

(10 marks)

Stretch and challenge

6 The following statements about breathing in (inhaling) are in the wrong order. Reorganise them to describe the process in the correct sequence.

air moves in to fill the lungs

air pressure in the lungs decreases

diaphragm moves down

diaphragm muscle contracts

intercostal muscles contract

ribcage moves up and out

volume in the lungs increases

intercostal muscles contract
↓
☐
↓
☐
↓
☐
↓
☐
↓
☐
↓
☐

(3 marks)

■ *Exam focus*

1 Which set of statements is correct? Circle the letter of the correct answer.

	Process	Carbon dioxide	Energy
A	photosynthesis	produces carbon dioxide	traps energy
B	photosynthesis	uses carbon dioxide	releases energy
C	aerobic respiration	uses carbon dioxide	releases energy
D	anaerobic respiration in muscles	produces no carbon dioxide	releases energy

[1]

2 The diagram shows a section through a human thorax (chest), including organs associated with breathing, gas exchange and circulation.

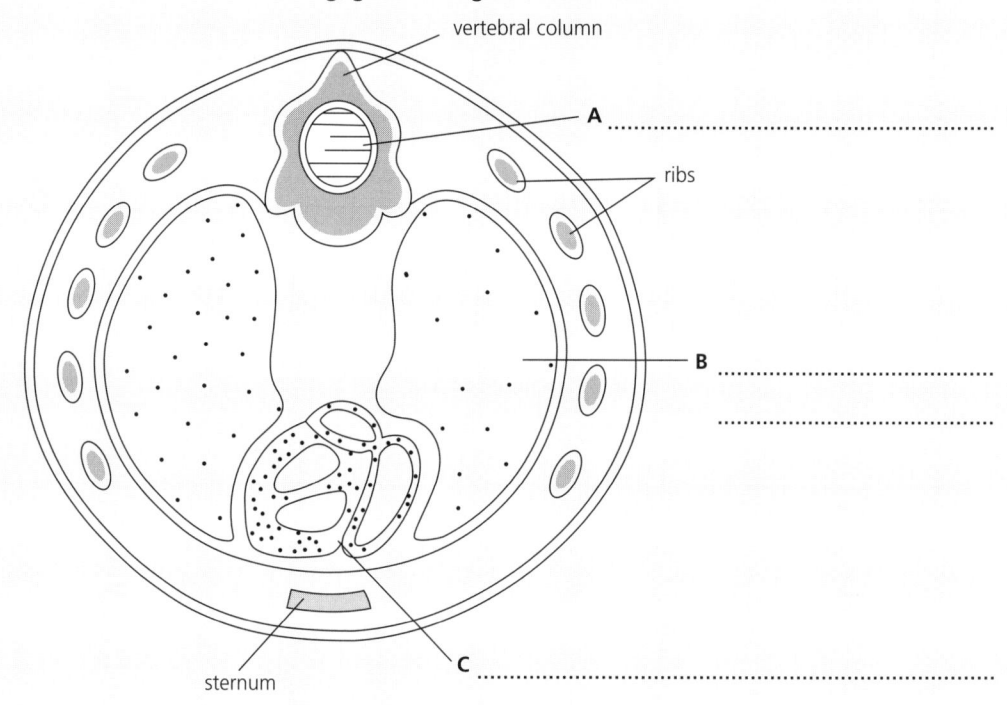

(a) On the diagram, identify the parts labelled **A**, **B** and **C**. [3]

(b) (i) State which organ shown in the diagram has the largest surface area.

....[1]

(ii) With reference to structures inside the organ, explain the importance of this large surface area.

....
....
....
....[4]

(c) Outline the role of the ribs, intercostal muscles and diaphragm in breathing in (inspiration).

....
....
....
....
....
.... [6]

[Total: 14]

3 (a) Describe the effects of physical activity on breathing.

....
....
....
.... [4]

(b) Name **three** chemicals present in cigarette smoke and outline their effects on the human body.

....
....
....
....
....
....
....
....
.... [9]

[Total: 13]

4 A conical flask was set up with a mixture of yeast and sugar solution, as shown in the diagram.

71

The amount of bubbling was observed and the gas given off was passed through limewater. The time taken for the limewater to change colour was recorded.
The experiment was carried out at five different temperatures. The results are shown in the table below.

Temperature/°C	Observation of bubbles	Time taken for limewater to change colour/s
0	no bubbles	no change
15	slow bubbling	320
30	many bubbles	65
45	slow bubbling	400
100	no bubbles	no change

(a) (i) Name the process carried out by the yeast to produce the bubbles of gas.

....[1]

(ii) What gas is tested for using limewater?

....[1]

(iii) State the colour change of the limewater, if this gas is present.

....[1]

(iv) Name a chemical that would be present in the flask at the end of the experiment at 30 °C but was **not** present at the start.

....[1]

(b) Outline what conclusions can be drawn from the results of these experiments.

....

....

....

....

....

....

....[5]

[Total: 9]

16 Excretion in humans

1 Complete the paragraph about the function of the kidney, using words from the list.

> active uptake   ADH   blood   concentrated   diffusion   dilute
> glucose   insulin   less   more   osmosis   reabsorbed   water

The kidney filters ...., removing urea, excess ....

and some mineral salts. All the .... is also filtered out, but it is all

.... Some water is also reabsorbed, depending on the state of

hydration of the body. This process is controlled by the hormone ....

On a hot day .... water is reabsorbed, resulting in a small amount

of .... urine. Water is reabsorbed by the process of ....,

while glucose and mineral salts are returned to the blood by .... and

....

(10 marks)

2 (a) Define the term *excretion*.

....

.... (2 marks)

(b) When urea is excreted, it passes through a number of structures before it is released as urine. Put the structures in the correct order, starting with the aorta.

> bladder   capillary   nephron   renal artery   ureter   urethra

aorta → ☐ → ☐ → ☐

☐ ← ☐ ← ☐ ← ☐

(3 marks)

3 (a) Describe how the level of amino acids is controlled in the body.

....

....

.... (3 marks)

(b) State **three** functions of the liver, other than the control of amino acid levels.

1 ....

2 ....

3 .... (3 marks)

Stretch and challenge

4 State **two** advantages and **two** disadvantages of kidney transplants compared with dialysis.

Advantage 1 ....

....

Advantage 2 ....

....

Disadvantage 1 ....

....

Disadvantage 2 ....

.... **(4 marks)**

■ *Exam focus*

1 The diagram shows the urinary system.

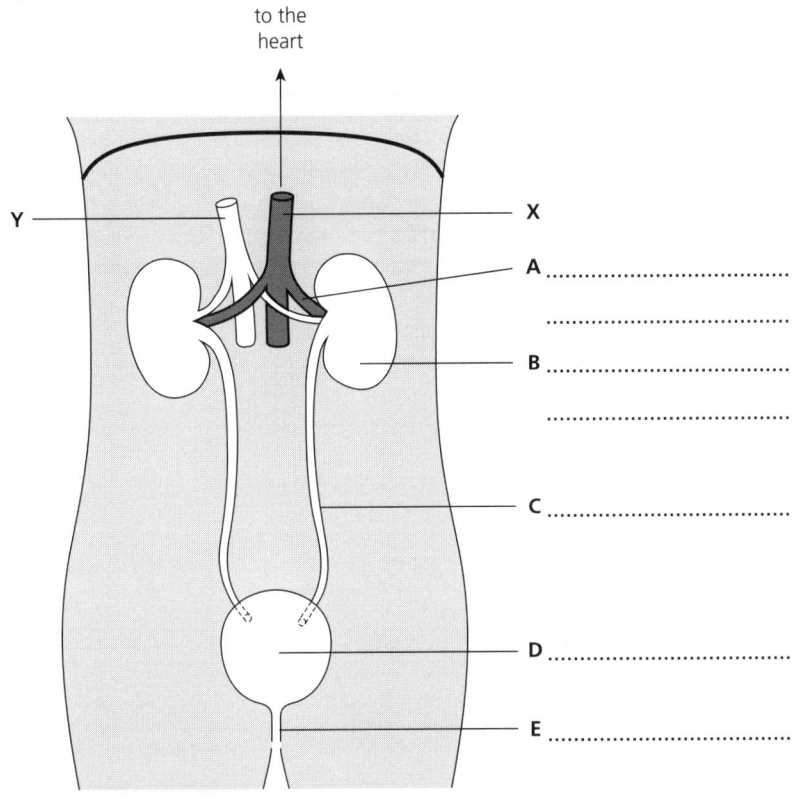

(a) (i) On the diagram, label parts **A–E**. [5]
   (ii) State **three** ways in which the substances *in solution* in part **A** would be different from those in part **C**.

   1 ....

   2 ....

   3 .... [3]

   (iii) Suggest how the contents of part **D** would be different on a hot day compared to a cold day.

   ....

   .... [2]

(b) State **three** differences between the structure of blood vessels **X** and **Y**.

   1 ....

   2 ....

   3 .... [3]

   [Total: 13]

2 The diagram shows a kidney machine.

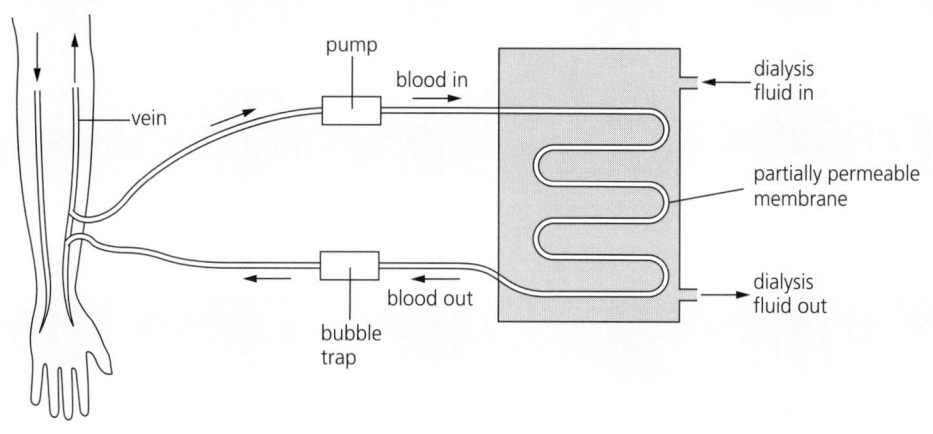

(a) (i) Explain the term *dialysis*.

....

.... [2]

(ii) Complete the table to outline the reasons for having the labelled parts in the kidney machine.

Part	Reason
pump	
dialysis fluid	
bubble trap	
partially permeable membrane	

[5]

(b) (i) Suggest a suitable material for the partially permeable membrane.

.... [1]

(ii) Explain why the membrane needs to be very long. ....

.... [2]

(iii) Explain why the bathing fluid needs to be changed regularly.

....

.... [2]

(c) State **two** disadvantages of using kidney machines.

1 ....

2 .... [2]

[Total: 14]

17 Reactions to stimuli by plants and invertebrates

1 (a) Define the term *geotropism*.

.... (1 mark)

(b) Complete the table by stating:
  (i) which part of a plant you would expect to grow towards gravity and which part would grow away from gravity
  (ii) an advantage to the growth response.

	Advantage of the growth response
part growing towards gravity	
part growing away from gravity	

(4 marks)

2 (a) State the term used to describe simple animal reactions to stimuli.

.... (1 mark)

(b) When given a choice, small invertebrates such as woodlice prefer to stay in damp, dark conditions. Suggest an advantage to woodlice of living in:

  (i) dark conditions ....

  (ii) damp conditions. .... (2 marks)

(c) Simple responses shown by woodlice are non-directional. Suggest how these animals find, and stay in, conditions they favour most, if they are not directly attracted to them.

....

....

.... (2 marks)

Stretch and challenge

3 (a) Name the chemical found in plants, which controls phototropism.

.... (1 mark)

(b) (i) State the effect of shining one-sided light onto a plant shoot.

.... (1 mark)

(ii) Explain how this effect is achieved in a shoot.

....

....

....

....

.... (4 marks)

(c) (i) Define the term *herbicide*.

.... (1 mark)

(ii) Describe and explain how synthetic plant hormones can be used as herbicides.

....

....

.... (3 marks)

■ *Exam focus*

1 The diagram shows a choice chamber, set up to investigate the responses of woodlice (small invertebrates) to four different conditions. The woodlice were supported on a fine mesh grill above the drying agent or the water.

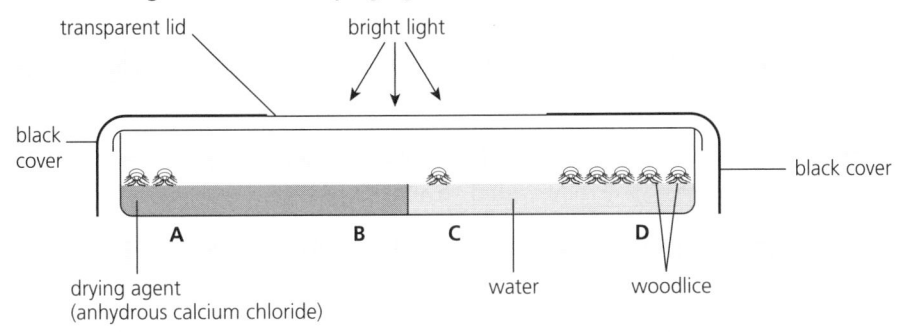

```
     transparent lid        bright light
                             ↓  ↓  ↓
black                                                        black cover
cover
          A          B         C          D
     drying agent              water    woodlice
     (anhydrous calcium chloride)
```

Thirty woodlice were placed in the centre of the choice chamber and allowed to move about for 5 minutes. Then the number of animals in each area was counted.
This process was carried out five times. The results are shown below.

Experiment	Number of woodlice in area			
	A	B	C	D
1	3	0	5	22
2	6	0	8	16
3	1	1	6	22
4	2	2	3	23
5	4	1	5	20
mean number				

(a) (i) Complete the table by calculating the mean number of woodlice in each area. [2]

(ii) State the conditions which would be achieved in each of the areas.

A .... and ....

B .... and ....

C .... and ....

D .... and .... [2]

(iii) Describe the conditions in which:

1 the most woodlice were found

.... [1]

2 the fewest woodlice were found.

.... [1]

(iv) Name the behavioural response shown by the woodlice.

.... [1]

(v) Suggest **two** advantages to the woodlice of choosing to stay in an area with the same conditions as area **D**.

1 ....

2 .... [2]

(b) (i) This investigation was carried out five times and then a mean was calculated. Suggest why this is important.

.... [1]

(ii) The woodlice were only left in the choice chamber for 5 minutes before being counted. Suggest why they should have been left for longer.

.... [1]

(iii) Suggest why the woodlice were supported on a fine mesh grill.

.... [1]

[Total: 12]

18 Coordination and response

1 (a) Distinguish between the central nervous system and the peripheral nervous system.

....

....

....

.... **(2 marks)**

(b) (i) Define the term *sense organ*.

....

.... **(2 marks)**

(ii) Complete the table by giving examples of sense organs and the stimuli they detect.

Sense organ	Stimulus detected
1 ear	
2	light
3 nose	
4	chemicals (taste)
5	temperature, pressure, touch, pain

(5 marks)

2 (a) State **three** differences between a sensory neurone and a motor neurone.

1 ....

2 ....

3 .... **(3 marks)**

(b) State the function for each of the following parts of a neurone.

1 myelin sheath ....

2 dendrite...

3 axon ....

4 cell body .... **(4 marks)**

3 (a) Define the term *hormone*.

....

.... **(2 marks)**

(b) A man experiences a sudden loud bang. This results in the secretion of adrenaline. Outline the effects of the adrenaline secretion on his body.

....

....

.... **(3 marks)**

(c) Complete the table to compare the nervous and hormonal control systems.

Feature	Nervous	Hormonal (endocrine)
form of transmission		
transmission pathway		
speed of transmission		
duration of effect		

(4 marks)

4 The diagram below shows a reflex arc involving a finger and arm.

.... **B**   ganglion
....   pain receptors
         spinal cord

.... **C**

A...

D...

(a) On the diagram:
  (i) identify neurones **A**, **B** and **C**   **(3 marks)**
  (ii) identify the effector **D**   **(1 mark)**
  (iii) add arrows to show the direction of the nerve impulse.   **(1 mark)**

82

(b) State the effect on **D** of receiving the nerve impulse.

.... (1 mark)

(c) (i) Name the gap that links neurones **A** to **B**, and **B** to **C**.

.... (1 mark)

(ii) Name the chemical that allows the nerve impulse to be 'transmitted' across the gap.

.... (1 mark)

5 The diagram shows a section through part of the eye.

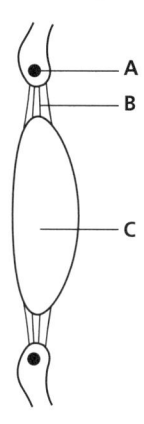

The parts labelled **A**, **B** and **C** are adjusted for distant vision.

(a) On the table, identify parts **A**, **B** and **C** and describe what would happen to each part if the eye was trying to focus on a near object.

Name of part	Description of action
A	
B	
C	

(6 marks)

(b) The diagram below shows an eye exposed to bright light.

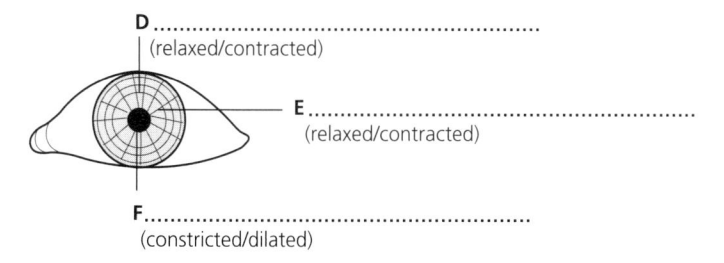

D ....
(relaxed/contracted)

E ....
(relaxed/contracted)

F ....
(constricted/dilated)

On the diagram:
(i) identify parts **D**, **E** and **F** (3 marks)
(ii) complete the annotation by crossing out the incorrect statements. (3 marks)

6 (a) Define the term *homeostasis*.

.... (2 marks)

(b) (i) State the normal human core body temperature. .... °C   (1 mark)

(ii) Outline **two** mechanisms the body uses to reduce its temperature to normal when it gets too hot.

1 ....

....

....

2 ....

....

.... (6 marks)

Stretch and challenge

7 (a) (i) Define the term *involuntary action*.

.... (1 mark)

(ii) How is the speed of an involuntary action different from the speed of a voluntary action?

.... (1 mark)

(iii) State **two** activities inside the body that are controlled involuntarily.

1 ....

2 .... (2 marks)

(b) Describe how blood sugar levels are returned to normal when they drop during a period of physical exercise.

....

....

....

.... (4 marks)

■ *Exam focus*

1 The diagram shows a cell.

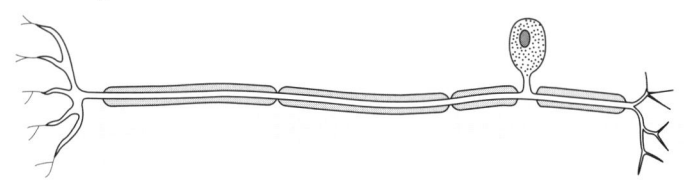

   What type of cell is shown? Circle the letter of the correct answer.
   A relay neurone
   B motor neurone
   C sensory neurone
   D cone cell   [1]

2 Drugs can be used legally, as medicines, but some drugs are misused and can have dangerous side-effects.
   (a) State **three** useful effects of drugs when used as medicines.

   1 ....

   2 ....

   3 .... [3]

   (b) (i) Complete the table to outline the effects and dangers of three drugs.

Drug	Effects on the body	Dangers to the person using the drug
alcohol		
heroin		
nicotine (in tobacco)		

[6]

   (ii) Using a drug such as alcohol or heroin can also have social effects. Outline the problems that can be caused.

   ....

   ....

   ....[3]

   [Total: 12]

85

3 With reference to glucose levels in the blood, describe the role of negative feedback in homeostasis.

....
....
....
....
....
....
....
.... [8]

4 The diagram shows the muscles and bones in the arm.

A ....
B ....
C ....
F ....
D ....
E ....

(a) (i) On the diagram, label parts **A–F**. [6]

   (ii) State the type of tissue that connects part **C** to part **D**. .... [1]

(b) (i) Parts **C** and **F** are called effectors and they are also antagonistic muscles. Define the terms *effector* and *antagonistic muscle*.

   Effector ....

   ....

   Antagonistic muscle..

   .... [3]

   (ii) Explain how the arm would be straightened. ....

   .... [2]

   (iii) Describe what happens to part **C** during this process.

   .... [1]

   [Total: 13]

19 Reproduction, growth and development in plants

1 **(a)** Define the term *asexual reproduction*.

    ....

    .... (2 marks)

(b) Outline how the named organisms reproduce.

  (i) Bacteria ....

    ....

    ....

    ....

  (ii) Fungi ....

    ....

    ....

    ....

  (iii) Potato ....

    ....

    ....

    ....(9 marks)

2 Draw line to match each of the parts of the flower to its function.

Flower part	Function
anther	protects the flower while in bud
ovary	often large and coloured to attract insects
petal	produces pollen grains containing male sex cells
sepal	sticky, to receive pollen grains during pollination
stigma	contains ovules, the female sex cells

(5 marks)

3 The diagram shows a section through the reproductive parts of an insect-pollinated flower.

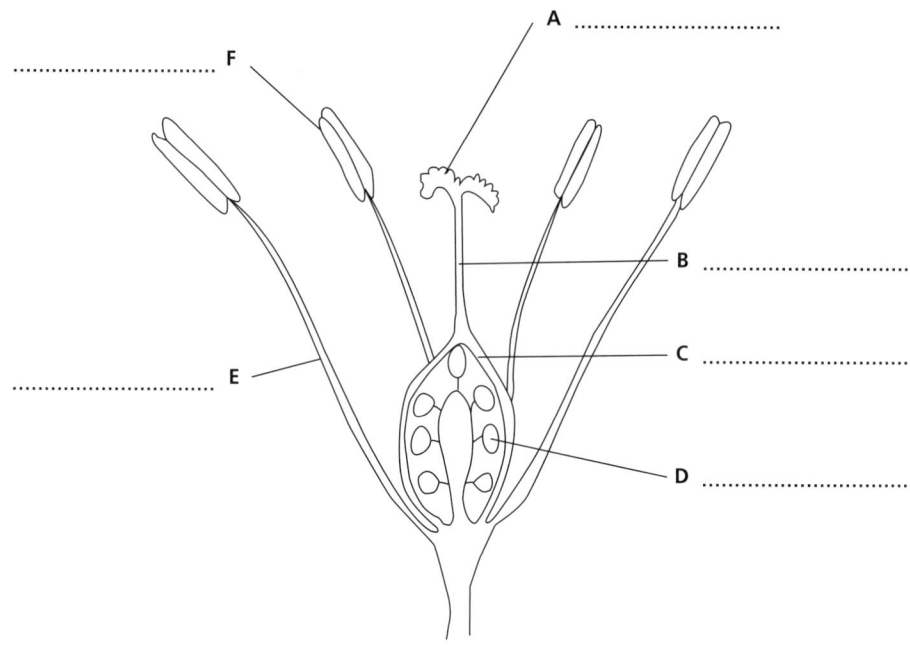

(i) On the diagram, label parts **A–F**. (6 marks)

(ii) Name the reproductive structures made up of:

   1 parts **A**, **B** and **C** .... (1 mark)

   2 parts **E** and **F**. .... (1 mark)

(iii) Suggest and explain how the following would be different in a wind-pollinated flower.

   1 Part **A**.

   ....

   .... (2 marks)

   2 The contents of part **F**

   ....

   .... (2 marks)

4 (a) Distinguish between the terms *growth* and *development*.

   ....

   ....

   ....

   .... (4 marks)

(b) Outline how a named seed is:
  (i) adapted for wind dispersal

  name of seed ....

  adaptation

  ....

  .... (2 marks)

  (ii) adapted for animal dispersal.

  name of seed ....

  adaptation

  ....

  .... (2 marks)

(c) Explain why each of the following environmental conditions is necessary for seed germination.
  (i) Oxygen

  ....

  ....

  (ii) Suitable temperature

  ....

  ....

  (iii) Water

  ....

  .... (6 marks)

(d) Explain why there is:
  (i) a drop in dry mass of a seed when it germinates

  ....

  .... (2 marks)

  (ii) an increase in dry mass once the plumule has grown through the soil.

  ....

  .... (2 marks)

Stretch and challenge

5 (a) State **two** advantages and **two** disadvantages of sexual reproduction in plants.

Advantage 1 ....

Advantage 2 ....

Disadvantage 1 ....

Disadvantage 2 .... **(4 marks)**

(b) Complete the table to compare self-pollination and cross-pollination.

	Definition	**Advantage**	**Disadvantage**
self-pollination			
cross-pollination			

(6 marks)

■ *Exam focus*

1 The diagram shows a section through some of the reproductive parts of an insect-pollinated flower.

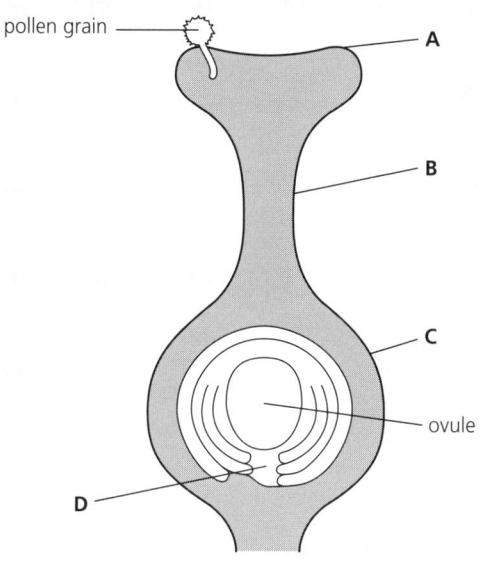

(a) (i) On the diagram, draw the route taken by the pollen grain to fertilise the ovule. [3]

(ii) Describe how the pollen grain achieves fertilisation. Refer to the labelled parts in your answer.

....

....

....

....

....

.... [6]

(b) The diagram above represents part of an insect-pollinated flower. Suggest how the following parts would be different in a wind-pollinated flower.

(i) The pollen grain

.... [1]

(ii) Part **A**

.... [2]

[Total: 12]

2 The diagram shows the structure of a flower.

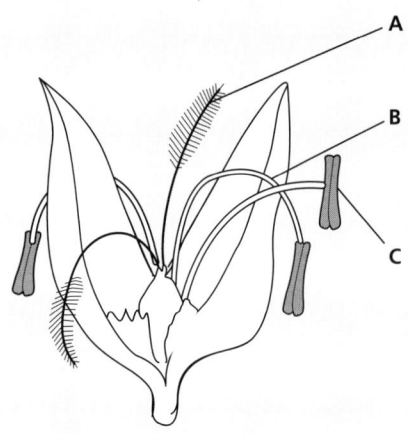

(a) State the type of pollination that this flower is adapted for. With reference to parts **A**, **B** and **C** explain your answer.

Type of pollination ....

Explanation ....

....

....

....

....

.... [7]

(b) Outline how the process of pollination happens in this flower.

....

....

....

.... [4]

[Total: 11]

20 Reproduction, growth and development in animals

1 Complete the crossword puzzle about the male reproductive system, using the clues to help you.

Across
2 adds fluid and nutrients to sperm, to form semen (8,5)
5 found in pairs, adding fluid to sperm (7,7)
6 male gonad that produces sperm (6)
7 tube linking the testis to urethra to carry semen (5,4)
8 transfers sperm to the vagina during sexual intercourse (5)

Down
1 carries semen and urine through the penis (7)
3 a mass of tubes in which sperm are stored (10)
4 a sac holding the testes outside the body (7)

(8 marks)

2 (a) Outline the route taken by a sperm during and after sexual intercourse, from the testes to a fertile egg.

....

....

....

.... **(6 marks)**

(b) Describe the process of fertilisation.

....

....

.... **(2 marks)**

3 The diagram shows the menstrual cycle, with the levels of two hormones and their effect on the lining of the uterus.

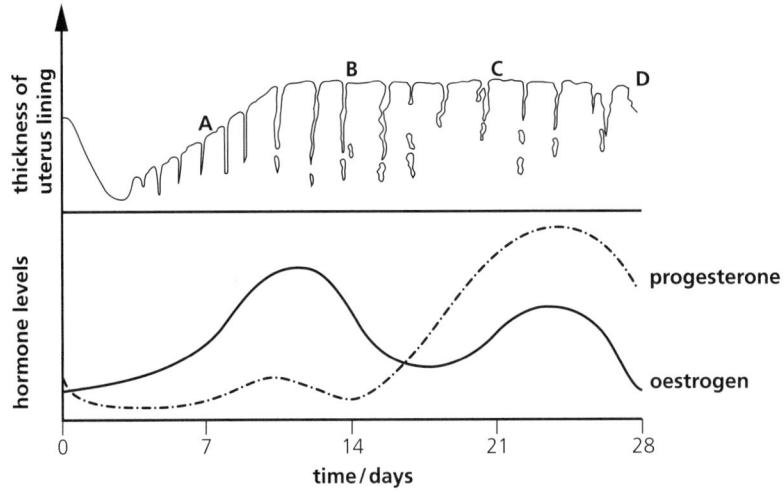

Describe what is happening at points **A**, **B**, **C** and **D**, referring to the causes of these events.

....

....

....

....

....

....

.... **(8 marks)**

4 Name each of the following, using their descriptions.

(a) The temporary structure that forms between the embryo and the lining of the uterus. ....

(b) The structures the baby passes through during birth.

  1 ....

  2 ....

(c) A fertilised egg, before it starts dividing. ....

(d) Two substances passed from the mother to the fetus.

  1 ....

  2 ....

(e) Two substances passed from the fetus to the mother.

  1 ....

  2 ....

(f) The liquid that acts as a shock absorber for the fetus. ....

(g) The process of shedding the uterus lining, along with blood. ....

(h) The release of semen from the penis. ....

(i) The site of fertilisation. ....

(j) The process of cell division that results in the change from a zygote into a ball of cells. .... (10 marks)

5 (a) Outline how each of the following methods of birth control can prevent pregnancy.

   1 Condom

   ....

   ....

   2 Vasectomy

   ....

   ....

   3 Contraceptive pill

   ....

   ....

   4 Intra-uterine device (IUD)

   ....

   .... (8 marks)

(b) State which **one** of the methods listed in part **(a)** is effective in preventing the transmission of HIV. .... (1 mark)

(c) State **two** other ways of preventing the transmission of HIV.

   1 ....

   2 .... (2 marks)

Stretch and challenge

6 (a) Name **two** hormones that are used in fertility drugs.

   1 ....

   2 .... (2 marks)

(b) (i) Outline the process of *in vitro* fertilisation.

   ....

   ....

   ....

   ....

   .... (3 marks)

(ii) State **one** advantage and **one** disadvantage of this process.

   Advantage ....

   Disadvantage .... (2 marks)

■ *Exam focus*

1 The following are all associated with reproduction:

   | egg cell sperm cell ovule zygote |

   Which feature is **not** common to all of these? Circle the letter of the correct answer.

   A nucleus
   B cell membrane
   C cytoplasm
   D haploid number of chromosomes [1]

2 The diagram shows a fetus inside the uterus.

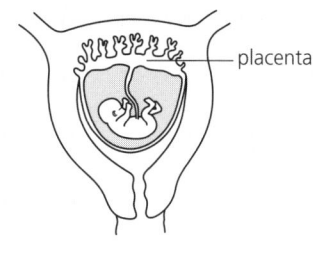

   Which statement about the placenta is **not** correct? Circle the letter of the correct answer.

   A It prevents viruses passing to the fetus.
   B It removes excretory products produced by the fetus.
   C It develops from the cells of the fetus.
   D It provides the fetus with oxygen. [1]

3 Distinguish between the following pairs of terms.

   (a) Testis and testa

   ....
   ....
   .... [4]

   (b) Urethra and ureter

   ....
   ....
   .... [3]

   (c) Ovary and ovule

   ....
   ....
   .... [4]

   (d) Fertilisation and implantation

   ....
   ....
   .... [4]

   [Total: 15]

4 (a) What type of organism causes each of the following diseases?

   AIDS ....

   Gonorrhoea .... [2]

(b) State which of the above diseases cannot be successfully treated with antibiotics.

   .... [1]

(c) Explain how dependency on a drug such as heroin can lead to infection with HIV.

   ....

   .... [2]

   [Total: 5]

5 The diagram shows a front view of the reproductive organs of a woman.

(a) On the diagram, label parts **A**, **B**, **C**, **D** and **E**. [5]

(b) State and explain what feature, shown on the diagram, indicates that this woman is infertile.

   Feature ....

   Explanation .... [2]

(c) The woman's infertility problem could be overcome by removing some eggs from her ovaries and fertilising them in a Petri dish.
   (i) State the name of this type of fertilisation.

   .... [1]

   (ii) Place an **X** on the diagram to show where a fertilised ovum should be implanted. [1]
   (iii) State **two** disadvantages of this type of treatment.

   1 ....

   2 .... [2]

(d) After successful implantation, pregnancy has been achieved. Outline **three** aspects of ante-natal care to maintain the development and growth of the fetus.

   1 ....

   2 ....

   3 .... [3]

   [Total: 14]

21 Inheritance

1 Draw lines to match each of the genetic terms to its definition. **(7 marks)**

Genetic term	Definition
allele	a section of DNA, coding for a specific protein
chromosome	having a pair of identical alleles
dominant	a thread of DNA, made up of genes
gene	a gene that always shows in the phenotype
genotype	the characteristics visible in an organism
homozygous	an alternative form of a gene
phenotype	the genetic make-up of an organism

2 Complete the diagram below to show how sex is inherited.

Parent phenotype   male   female

Parent genotype   .... × ....

Gametes (sex cells)   ○   ○   ×   ○   ○

First filial
generation (F1)   ....

Phenotype   ....

The ratio is   .... female: .... male.   **(5 marks)**

3 (a) State **two** differences between the processes of mitosis and meiosis.

1 ....

2 .... **(2 marks)**

(b) A fruit fly has eight chromosomes in its body cells. Complete the table to show how many chromosomes would be present in the cells listed.

Type of cell	Number of chromosomes
leg muscle cell	
sperm cell	
zygote	
skin cell	

(4 marks)

(c) Fruit flies can have grey bodies or black bodies. Black body colour (g) is recessive to grey body colour (G). A pure-breeding grey fly was cross-bred with a pure-breeding black fly. The next (F1) generation were all grey bodied.
   (i) Construct a genetic cross to show how the F1 generation were all grey bodied.

(3 marks)

   (ii) Two flies from the F1 generation were cross-bred. Use a genetic cross to predict the genotypes and phenotypes of the next (F2) generation.

(4 marks)

Stretch and challenge

4 Snapdragon plants show codominance.
   (a) Explain the term *codominance*.

   ....
   ....
   .... (3 marks)

Pure-breeding snapdragon flowers can be red ($C^R C^R$) or white ($C^W C^W$).
   (b) (i) Use a genetic cross to show how pink snapdragon flowers could be formed from pure-breeding parents.

(4 marks)

   (ii) Some pink-flowering snapdragon plants were self-pollinated. Predict the ratio of red, pink and white flowers that would be achieved from this cross.

   .... (1 mark)

■ *Exam focus*

1 (a) (i) Explain why it is important not to mix different blood groups when a hospital patient is receiving a blood transfusion.

....

....

.... [3]

(ii) Suggest **one** other risk involved in blood transfusions.

.... [1]

(b) Use a genetic diagram to show how parents, neither of whom has blood group O, can have children that include the blood groups O and AB. Use the symbols I^A, I^B, and I^o to represent the alleles responsible for the human blood groups.

[5]
[Total: 9]

2 The diagram shows the results of some breeding experiments using rats.

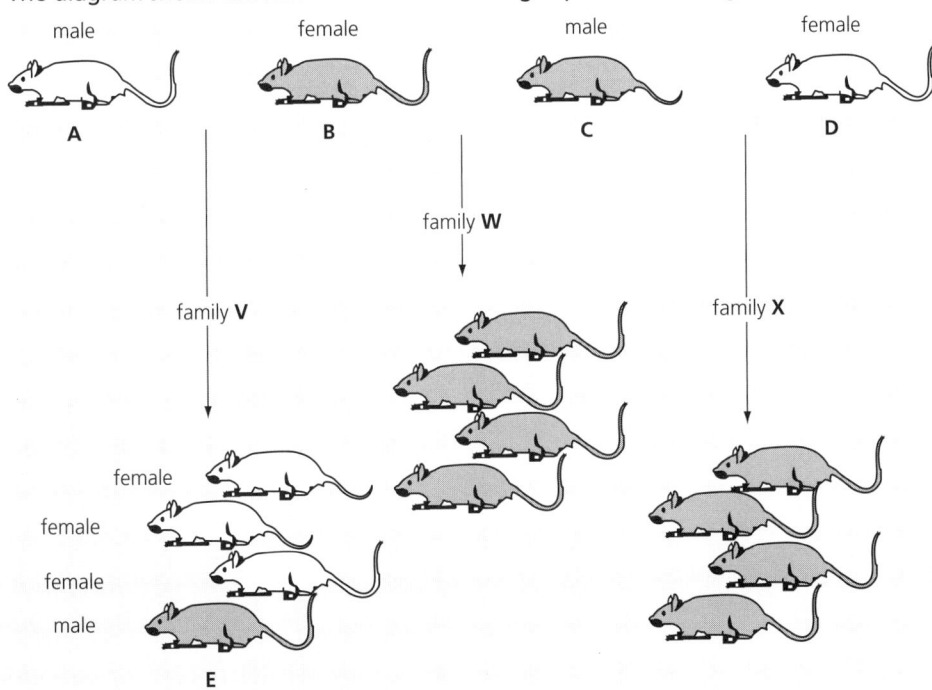

101

(a) (i) Complete the table to show the sex chromosomes present in the gametes of rats **B** and **C**.

Rat B		Rat C	

[1]

(ii) If rats **B** and **C** had a second family, what is the percentage chance that the first rat born would be male?

.... [1]

(iii) Which sex cell determines the sex of the baby rat? Explain your answer.

....

....[2]

(b) Coat colour in these rats is controlled by a single pair of alleles showing complete dominance.

(i) Define the term *allele*.

....

....[2]

(ii) Which of the parent mice **A–D** is likely to be:

   1 homozygous dominant for coat colour? .... [1]

   2 heterozygous for coat colour? .... [1]

(c) Rat **E** was later cross-bred with a rat of the same genotype as its mother (rat **B**). Write out a genetic cross to show how coat colour would be inherited in this family.

[5]
[Total: 13]

3 Distinguish between the following pairs of genetic terms.

(a) *Gene* and *allele*

....

....

....[2]

(b) *Diploid* and *haploid*

....

....

....[2]

(c) *Phenotype* and *genotype*

....

....

....[2]

(d) *Homozygous* and *heterozygous*

....

....

....[2]

(e) *Dominant* and *recessive*

....

....

....[2]

[Total: 10]

22 Variation

1 (a) (i) Define the term *mutation*.

.... (1 mark)

(ii) State **two** causes of mutations.

1 ....

2 .... (2 marks)

(b) Down's syndrome is a result of a mutation.

(i) Outline how Down's syndrome occurs.

....

....

....

.... (3 marks)

(ii) Describe the characteristics of a Down's syndrome child.

....

....

.... (3 marks)

2 (a) Using examples, distinguish between continuous variation and discontinuous variation. In each case, state their causes.

....

....

....

....

....

....

....

.... (6 marks)

(b) Sketch graphs to illustrate the examples used in your answer.

(2 marks)

3 Describe how artificial selection can be used to produce a named variety of animal with increased economic importance.

....
....
....
....
.... (4 marks)

Stretch and challenge

4 (a) Define the term *natural selection*. ....
.... (2 marks)

(b) Using a named example, outline how natural selection may lead to evolution.

....
....
....
....
....
....
.... (5 marks)

5 (a) Describe the symptoms of sickle cell anaemia.

....
.... (3 marks)

Stretch and challenge

(b) (i) A man and women are both heterozygous for sickle cell anaemia, each having the same genotype H^NH^n.

Complete the genetic cross to show the genotypes and phenotypes of their children.

Parents   man   woman

Parent genotype   ....   ×   ....

Gametes (sex cells)   ○   ○   ×   ○   ○

Genotype of first filial generation (F1)   □   □   □   □

Phenotype   ....

....

....   **(4 marks)**

(ii) Using a pencil, shade in the F1 genotype box(es) to show which of the children are most at risk of dying from sickle cell anaemia. **(1 mark)**

Exam focus

1 (a) (i) State the type of variation shown by human blood groups.

.... [1]

(ii) State an example of a different type of variation and explain how it is brought about.

Example ....

Explanation ....

.... [3]

(b) (i) Explain how a person who is heterozygous for sickle cell anaemia has protection from malaria.

....

.... [2]

(ii) Suggest why people who are homozygous recessive for sickle cell anaemia are at greater risk of dying, even though they have protection from malaria.

....

.... [2]

[Total: 8]

2 (a) Outline how cross-pollination can lead to variation in a species.

....

....

.... [3]

(b) Explain why a potato plant grown from a tuber will have identical characteristics to the plant that produced the tuber.

....

.... [2]

[Total: 5]

3 The diagram shows organism **X**.

1 micron

flagella   slime capsule

(a) (i) Identify what type of organism is shown in the diagram.................................. [1]

(ii) State **three** reasons for your answer.

1 ....

2 ....

3 .... [3]

(b) The diagram shows how the reproduction of organism **X** is affected by an antibiotic.

generation 1 — organism **X**

2

treatment with antibiotic

3 — organism **Y**

4

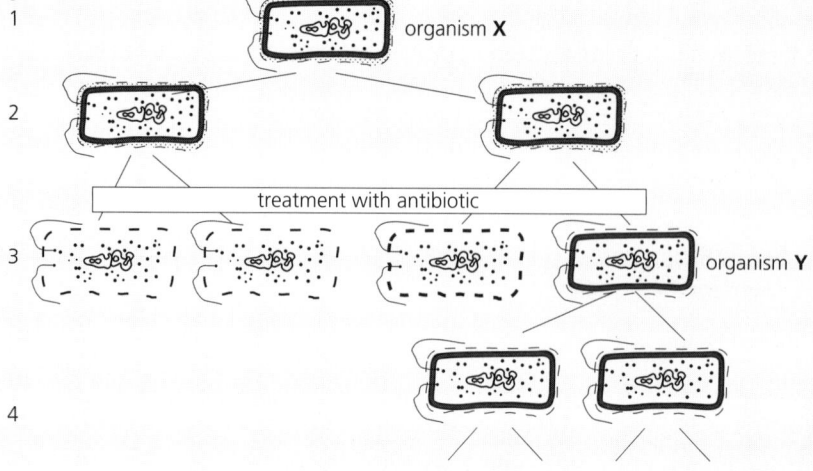

State the type of reproduction shown by organism **X**. .... [1]

(c) Organism **Y** has survived the antibiotic treatment, but the other organisms in the third generation have been killed.

Suggest why organism **Y** and its offspring in generation 4 have survived the antibiotic treatment.

....

.... [2]

(d) Explain why patients taking a 7-day course of antibiotics are advised to complete the full treatment, even though they may feel better after 3 or 4 days.

....

....

....

....

.... [3]

[Total: 10]

23 Energy flow, food chains and food webs

1 A bird of prey called a sparrow hawk hunts in a field of clover plants, searching for its prey – another bird called a thrush. The thrushes visit the field to feed on snails. The snails graze on the clover leaves.

   (a) Explain the meaning of the term *food chain*.

   ....

   .... (2 marks)

   (b) (i) Draw a food chain using the organisms described in the paragraph above.

   (3 marks)

   (ii) Add the following labels to the names of the organisms in the food chain.

   | primary consumer   producer   tertiary consumer   secondary consumer |

   (2 marks)

   (c) A farmer sprayed the clover field with a molluscicide, killing all the snails. Suggest and explain the effects of this treatment on:

   (i) thrushes

   ....

   .... (2 marks)

   (ii) sparrow hawks.

   ....

   .... (2 marks)

   (d) Suggest why the percentage energy lost at the snail trophic level of the food chain is less than that lost at the thrush trophic level.

   ....

   .... (2 marks)

109

2 (a) Plants form the first trophic level of food chains.

   (i) State the process used by plants to obtain their energy.

   .... (1 mark)

   (ii) What is the source of this energy? .... (1 mark)

   (iii) Give **three** reasons why plants do not make use of all the energy available to them.

   1 ....

   2 ....

   3 .... (3 marks)

(b) (i) Explain why there tend to be small numbers of top carnivores in a food chain.

   ....

   .... (2 marks)

   (ii) Explain why short food chains are more efficient than long food chains.

   ....

   .... (2 marks)

3 The diagram below shows a food web.

```
                 leopard
                  ↗  ↖
              baboon
                ↑           impala
             scorpion         ↑
                ↑
              locust
                 ↖  grass ↗
```

(a) In the boxes provided, state the trophic level of each of the organisms, other than the leopard. **(5 marks)**

(b) Suggest why the leopard is difficult to label in this food web.

.... (1 mark)

(c) Food webs can easily become unbalanced by the death of the population of one organism. Suggest **three** causes of the death of a population.

1 ....

2 ....

3 .... (3 marks)

(d) The organisms in the food web are linked by arrows. Explain what the arrows represent.

.... (1 mark)

Stretch and challenge

4 The diagram shows an inverted pyramid of numbers.

```
        fleas
         owl
       blue tits
      caterpillars
         oak
         tree
```

(a) Explain why pyramids of numbers, like the one shown above, can be inverted.

....

.... (2 marks)

(b) Explain why pyramids of energy always have a normal pyramid shape.

.... (1 mark)

(c) Explain why the process of collecting data for pyramids of energy is destructive.

....

.... (2 marks)

Exam focus

1 (a) (i) Define the term *trophic level*. ....

.... [1]

(ii) Draw an example of a food chain involving **four** trophic levels.

[2]

(iii) Draw and label a pyramid of energy for your food chain.

[2]

Plants obtain their energy from sunlight. 60% of this light is the wrong wavelength, or is reflected off the surface of the leaf. Another 5% passes through the leaf without being captured.

(b) (i) Calculate the percentage of the light available that is captured by the leaf.

....

.... [1]

(ii) What feature is present on the surface of a leaf which could reflect the light?

.... [1]

(iii) The main tissue in a leaf responsible for capturing light is the palisade layer. Describe how cells in this layer are adapted for efficient absorption.

....

.... [2]

(c) As energy passes through the animals in the food chain, some is lost.

(i) State what percentage of energy is lost between trophic levels.

.... [1]

(ii) State **two** ways in which the energy available to an animal at the next trophic level is used or lost.

1 ....

2 .... [2]

[Total: 12]

2 The diagram shows the energy in two food chains, from which humans obtain their energy.

food chain **A**

100 000 kJ → maize → 3000 kJ → humans

food chain **B**

100 000 kJ → grass → 4000 kJ → cows → 200 kJ → humans

(a) (i) Label the trophic levels on the lines below food chain **B**. [3]

(ii) Outline how energy enters the food chain.

....

....

.... [3]

(iii) State **three** uses of energy by the cows in food chain **B**.

1 ....

2 ....

3 .... [3]

(b) (i) Calculate the percentage energy available in food chain **B** which is passed to humans.

.... [2]

(ii) Outline why food chain **A** is more efficient in providing energy for humans.

....

.... [2]

(c) (i) Suggest why eating a mixed diet of animals and plants could be considered healthier than eating only plants.

....

.... [2]

(ii) Using the organisms in food chains A and B, draw a food web to show humans eating both maize and cows.

[3]

[Total: 18]

24 Nutrient cycles

1 State the **four** main processes involved in the carbon cycle.

   1 ....

   2 ....

   3 ....

   4 .... **(4 marks)**

2 The diagram shows the water cycle.

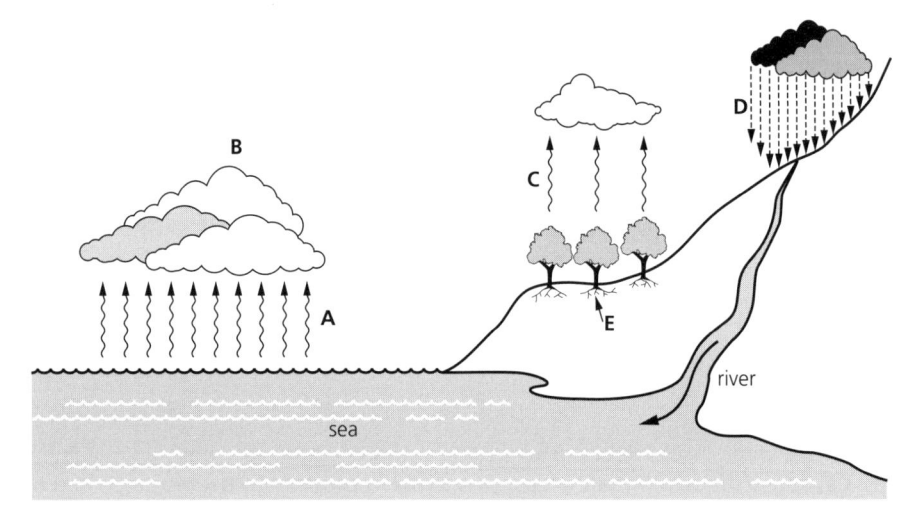

Identify the processes involved **A–E**.

A ....

B ....

C ....

D ....

E .... **(5 marks)**

Stretch and challenge

3 (a) Describe the roles of each of the following in the nitrogen cycle.

  (i) Nitrogen-fixing bacteria

  ....

  .... (2 marks)

  (ii) Nitrifying bacteria

  ....

  .... (2 marks)

  (iii) Denitrifying bacteria

  ....

  .... (2 marks)

  (iv) Lightning

  ....

  .... (2 marks)

(b) State **three** strategies that farmers can use to increase the concentration of nitrates in soil.

  1 ....

  2 ....

  3 .... (3 marks)

4 There is a delicate balance between the amounts of carbon dioxide and oxygen in the atmosphere.

(a) State the **two** processes, occurring in living things, which affect this balance.

  1 ....

  2 .... (2 marks)

(b) Describe **two** human activities which, when carried out on a large scale, can affect this balance.

  1 ....

  2 .... (2 marks)

(c) Outline why global warming is considered to be an environmental problem.

  ....

  ....

  ....

  ....

  ....

  .... (3 marks)

115

Exam focus

1 The diagram shows a bean, which is a leguminous plant, and maize, which is a non-leguminous plant. Both are growing in the same soil in a farmer's field.

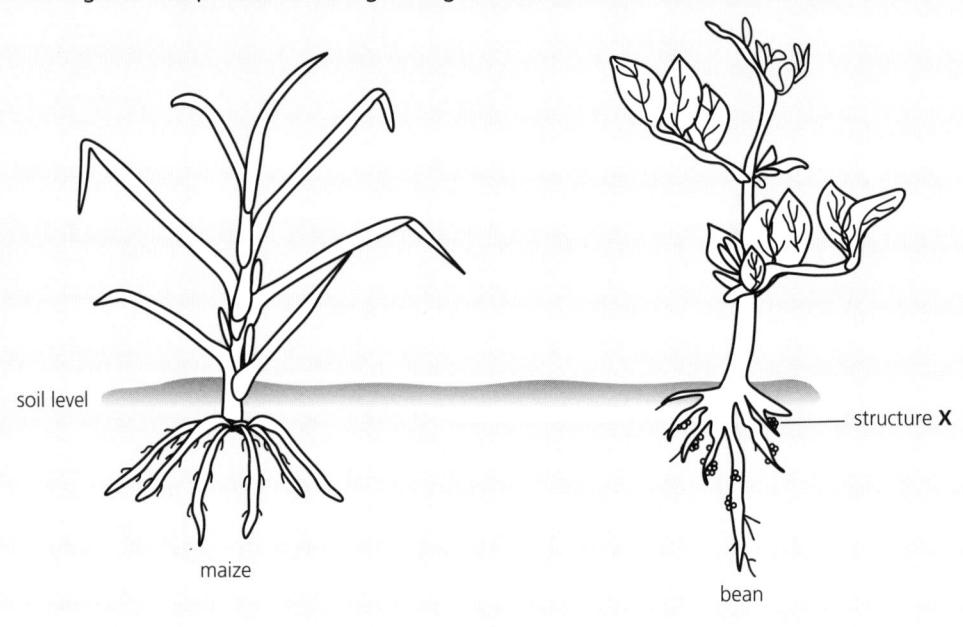

(a) (i) Identify structure **X**.

.... [1]

(ii) Structure **X** contains organisms. State the group to which they belong.

.... [1]

(iii) The bean plant grew better than the maize plant. The farmer tested the soil and found it was low in nitrates. Explain why the bean plant grew well, even though the nitrate levels were low.

....

....

....

.... [4]

(iv) Suggest **two** ways the farmer could improve the soil to help the maize plants to grow better.

1 ....

2 .... [2]

(b) Maize is a monocotyledon and the bean is a dicotyledon. Complete the table by identifying **two** features which help to classify these plants.

Feature	Maize	Bean
1		
2		

[3]

[Total: 11]

2 Describe how water molecules entering the roots of a mountain plant can eventually be found in the sea. Use terms relating to the water cycle in your answer.

....

....

....

....

....

....

.... [8]

25 Population size

1 (a) (i) On the axes below, sketch a graph to show a curve of population growth, influenced by limiting factors.

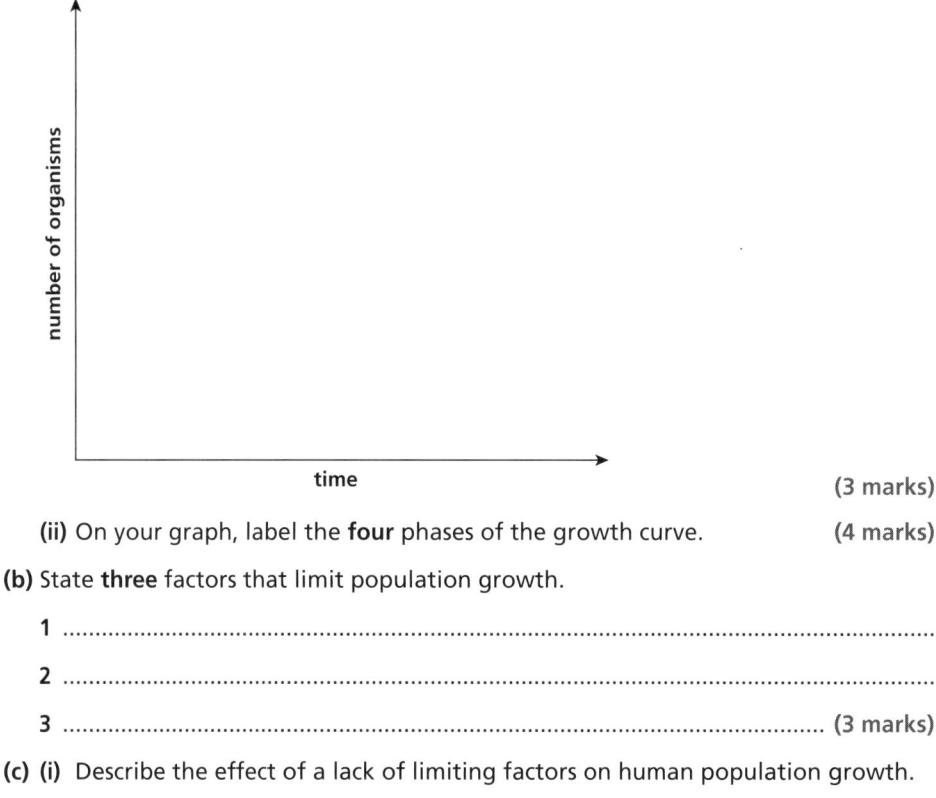

[graph axes: y-axis labelled "number of organisms", x-axis labelled "time"]

(3 marks)

(ii) On your graph, label the **four** phases of the growth curve. (4 marks)

(b) State **three** factors that limit population growth.

1 ....

2 ....

3 .... (3 marks)

(c) (i) Describe the effect of a lack of limiting factors on human population growth.

....

.... (2 marks)

(ii) Outline the social implications of this effect.

....

....

....

.... (4 marks)

Stretch and challenge

2 Describe and explain the shape of each of the phases of a human population curve.

....
....
....
....
....
....
....
....
....
....
....
....
.... **(8 marks)**

Exam focus

1 The graph below shows the population growth of yeast cells, kept in conditions with no limiting factors.

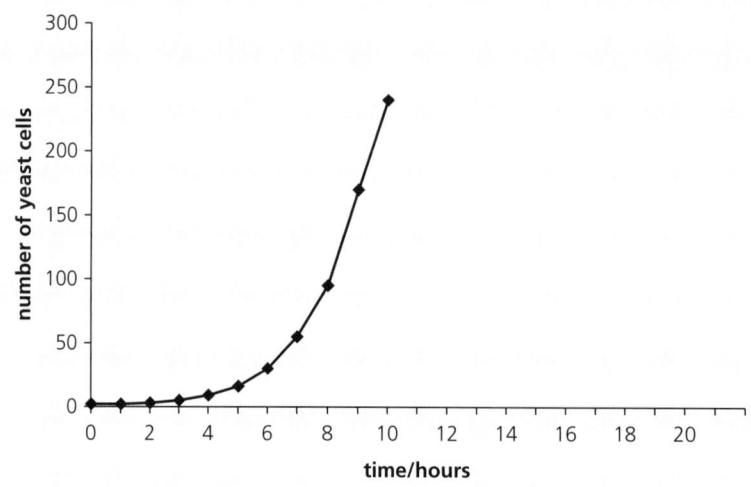

[Graph: number of yeast cells (y-axis, 0–300) vs time/hours (x-axis, 0–20). Curve remains near 0 until about hour 4, then rises steeply to ~240 at hour 10.]

(a) (i) On the graph, label:

    1 the lag phase [1]

    2 the log phase. [1]

  (ii) Explain why the lag phase and the log phase are the shapes shown.

    Lag phase ....

    ....

    Log phase ....

    .... [2]

(b) (i) Extend the line of the graph to represent what would happen to the yeast population if limiting factors started to have an effect. [2]

  (ii) Add labels on your line to name the extra phases of the growth curve. [2]

  (iii) State **three** factors that could limit the growth of the yeast cells.

    1 ....

    2 ....

    3 .... [3]

(c) It is very difficult to maintain a growing population of yeast cells without the cells eventually creating limiting factors.

Suggest **one** substance the yeast cells could produce to limit the growth of the population.

.... [1]

[Total: 12]

26 Human influences on the ecosystem

1 Explain **four** ways in which modern technology has been used to increase food production.

   1 ....
   ....
   2 ....
   ....
   3 ....
   ....
   4 ....
   .... **(8 marks)**

2 A logging company applied for permission to cut down a large area of forest. An environmental campaign group objected to the plan.

   (a) What term is used to describe the removal of large areas of forest?
   .... **(1 mark)**

   (b) Suggest **three** reasons why the logging company were planning to cut down the forest.

   1 ....
   2 ....
   3 .... **(3 marks)**

   (c) The environmental campaign group made a list of the undesirable effects on the environment of cutting down the trees and explained their possible consequences. Describe and explain four possible effects.

   1 ....
   ....
   2 ....
   ....
   3 ....
   ....
   4 ....
   .... **(8 marks)**

3 The following statements describe the process of eutrophication in a lake, caused by water pollution by fertilisers. They are in the wrong order. Reorganise them in the correct sequence, writing the letter for each stage in the boxes.

   A algae absorb fertiliser and grow rapidly (algal bloom)
   B algae die without light
   C fertilisers are very soluble and are easily leached out of the soil
   D animals in water die through lack of oxygen
   E algae form a blanket on the surface of the water, blocking light from the algae below
   F bacteria decompose dead algae, using up oxygen in the water for respiration
   G fertilisers are washed into the lake

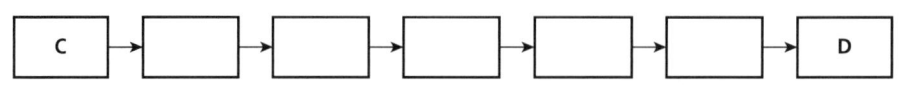

   C → ☐ → ☐ → ☐ → ☐ → ☐ → D

   (5 marks)

4 (a) Explain how the pollution of a lake by small amounts of a chemical waste such as a heavy metal can result in the death of animals at the top of the food chain.

   ....
   ....
   ....
   .... (4 marks)

   (b) (i) State **two** sources of sulfur dioxide.

   1 ....
   2 .... (2 marks)

   (ii) List **three** problems caused by acid rain, formed from sulfur dioxide.

   1 ....
   2 ....
   3 .... (3 marks)

Stretch and challenge

5 Outline the process of recycling sewage.

   ....
   ....
   ....
   ....
   ....
   .... (5 marks)

■ *Exam focus*

1 (a) Using an example familiar to you, describe the importance of conserving a species of animal that is under threat of extinction.

....

....

....

.... [4]

(b) For the species you have named:
  (i) describe the habitat it lives in

....

.... [2]

  (ii) outline how this habitat could be conserved to protect the species.

....

....

.... [3]

[Total: 9]

2 The diagram shows some human activities that can result in pollution entering a river.

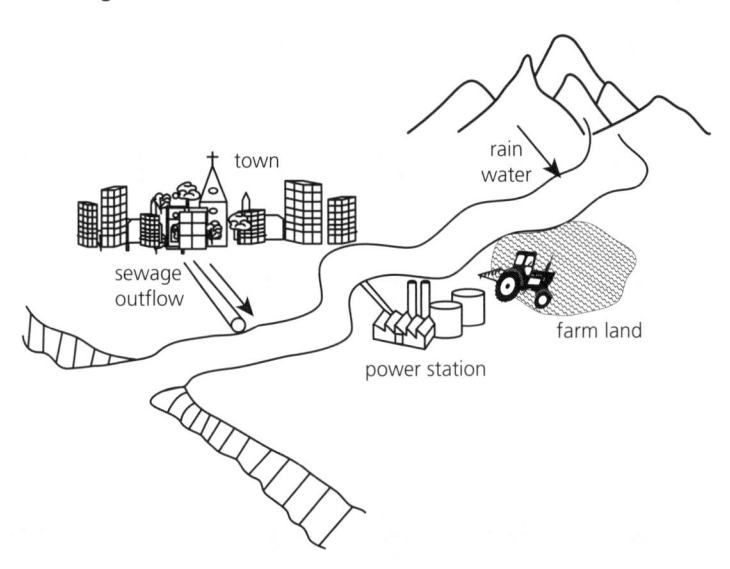

Outline and explain the harmful effects of each of the activities shown.
(a) Farming

....

....

....

....

.... [4]

(b) Power station

....
....
....
....
....
.... [4]

(c) Town

....
....
....
....
....
.... [4]

[Total: 12]

PAST EXAM QUESTIONS

1 The table shows some of the external features of the five classes of vertebrates.

Complete the table by using a tick (✓) to indicate if each class has the feature or a cross (×) if it does not. The first row has been completed for you.

Feature	Fish	Amphibia	Reptiles	Birds	Mammals
mammary glands	×	×	×	×	✓
fur / hair					
scales / scaly skin					
external ears					
feathers					

[Total: 4]

(Cambridge IGCSE Biology 0610, Paper 31 Q1 May/June 2009)

2 The figure shows six arthropods, each of which could carry disease organisms.

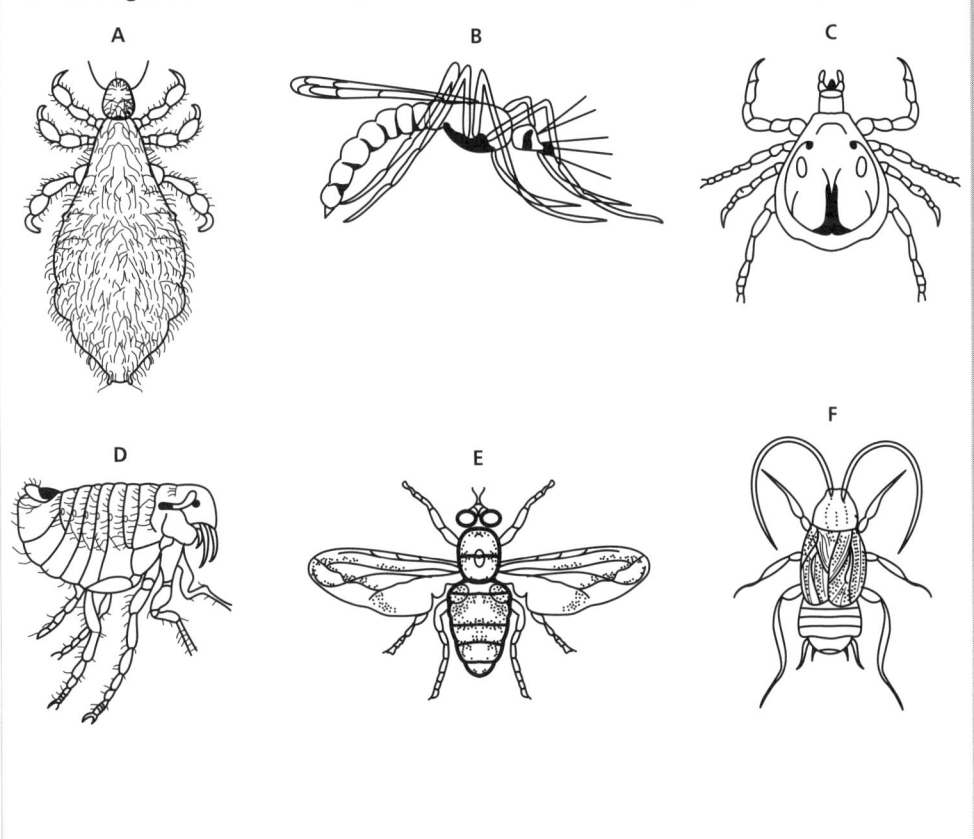

125

Use the key to identify each of the arthropods. Write the name of each arthropod in the correct box of the table. As you work through the key, tick (✓) the boxes in the table to show how you identified each arthropod.

Arthropod **A** has been completed for you as an example.

Key

	Arthropod
1 (a) Wings present	go to 2
(b) Wings absent	go to 4
2 (a) Wings shorter than abdomen	go to 3
(b) Wings longer than abdomen	*Musca*
3 (a) Abdomen long and narrow	*Anopheles*
(b) Abdomen short and broad	*Periplaneta*
4 (a) Has three pairs of legs	go to 5
(b) Has four pairs of legs	*Ornithodorus*
5 (a) One pair of legs shorter than the other pairs	*Pulex*
(b) All pairs of legs of similar length	*Pediculus*

	1 (a)	1 (b)	2 (a)	2 (b)	3 (a)	3 (b)	4 (a)	4 (b)	5 (a)	5 (b)	Name of arthropod
A		✓					✓			✓	*Pediculus*
B											
C											
D											
E											
F											

[Total: 5]

(Cambridge IGCSE Biology 0610, Paper 2 Q1 May/June 2009)

3 The figure shows *Euglena gracilis*, a single-celled organism, often found in freshwater ponds.

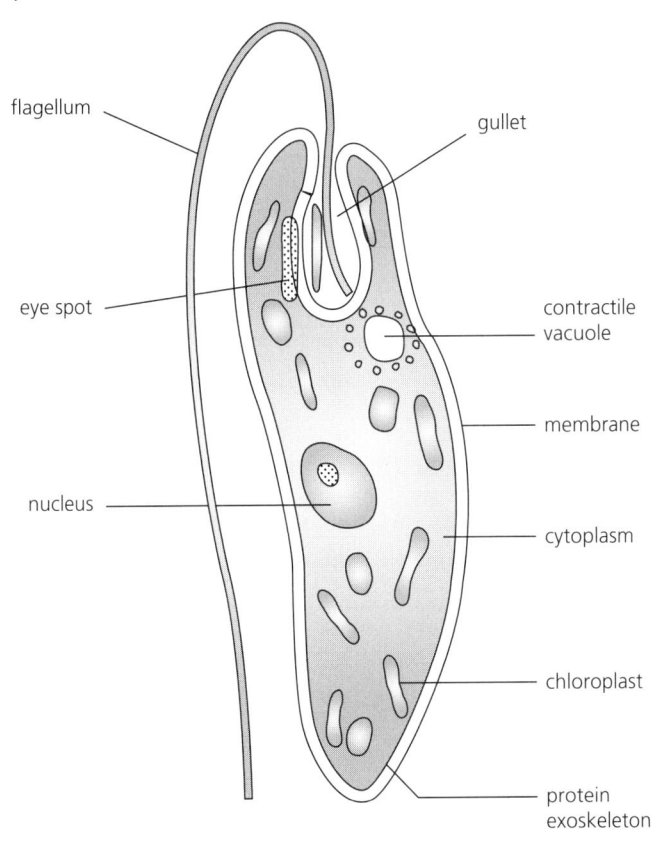

Euglena shows a number of the characteristics of living things such as excretion, nutrition and irritability.

(a) Name three other characteristics of living things that you would expect this organism to show.

1 ....

2 ....

3 .... [3]

(b) *Euglena* is difficult to classify because it shows animal characteristics and plant characteristics, some of which are listed in the table below. For each characteristic, identify it as an animal, plant or bacterial cell feature by putting a tick (✓) for present or a cross (✗) for absent in each box in the table.

Feature	Animal cell	Plant cell	Bacterial cell
chloroplast			
cytoplasm			
membrane			
nucleus			

[4]

(c) The cytoplasm of *Euglena* contains salts that are more concentrated than those in the surrounding water. The contractile vacuole excretes any excess water.
Explain why this function of the contractile vacuole is important to this organism.

....
....
....
.... [3]

(d) *Euglena* has an eye spot that is sensitive to light.
  (i) Suggest and explain how the organism would respond if there was an area of brighter light nearby.

....
....
....
.... [2]

  (ii) Explain how the organism would benefit from this reaction.

....
....
....
.... [2]

[Total: 14]

(Cambridge IGCSE Biology 0610, Paper 3 Q1 May/June 2001)

4 (a) Draw a straight line to match the diagram of each tissue with its function. The first has been completed for you.

- absorbs water and minerals from soil for the plant
- carries oxygen around the body of mammals
- contracts to cause movement within animals
- moves dust and bacteria up the bronchi of a mammal
- transports water and minerals through the stem of a plant

[4]

(b) Explain why a leaf is described as an organ, not a tissue.

....
....
....
....
.... [3]

[Total: 7]

(Adapted from Cambridge IGCSE Biology 0610, Paper 3 Q1 May/June 2006)

5 The figure shows four test-tubes that were set up and left for 6 hours at a constant warm temperature.

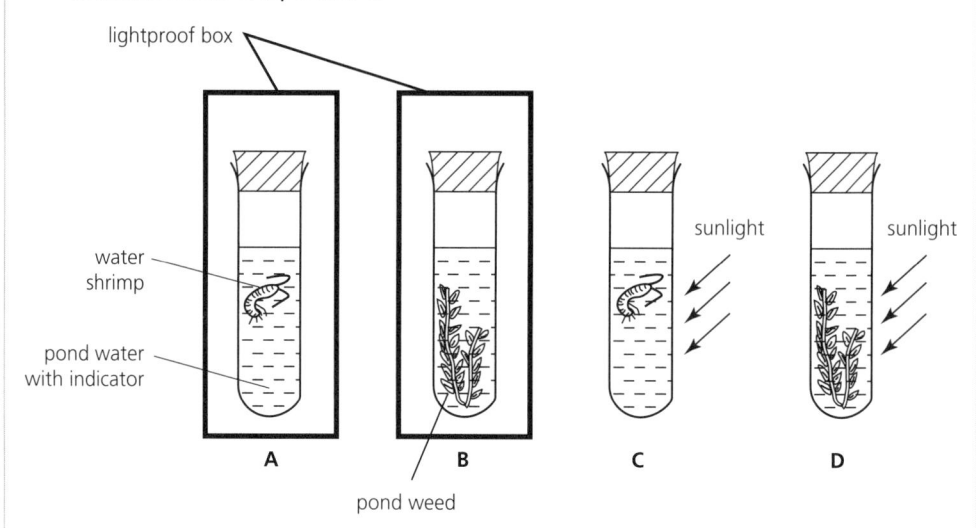

- lightproof box
- water shrimp
- pond water with indicator
- pond weed

A   B   C   D

Hydrogencarbonate indicator (bicarbonate indicator) changes colour depending on the pH of gases dissolved in it, as shown below.

concentration of carbon dioxide dissolved

high → low

pH 1	pH 7	pH 14
indicator yellow	indicator pinky red	indicator purple

After 6 hours the colour of the indicator in all four tubes had changed.
(a) (i) Complete the table to predict the colour of the indicator after 6 hours.

Tube	Colour of indicator at start	Colour of indicator after 6 hours
A	pinky red	
B	pinky red	
C	pinky red	
D	pinky red	

[4]

(ii) Suggest the reason for the change in colour of the indicator in each of tubes **A** and **D**.

Tube A...

....

....

Tube D...

....

.... [4]

(b) The figure shows a fifth tube, **E**, set up at the same time and in the same conditions as tubes **C** and **D**.

Suggest and explain the possible colour of the indicator in tube **E** after 6 hours.

Colour of indicator...

Explanation ....

....

....

.... [3]

[Total: 11]

(Cambridge IGCSE Biology 0610, Paper 2 Q6 May/June 2009)

6 The figure shows the water cycle.

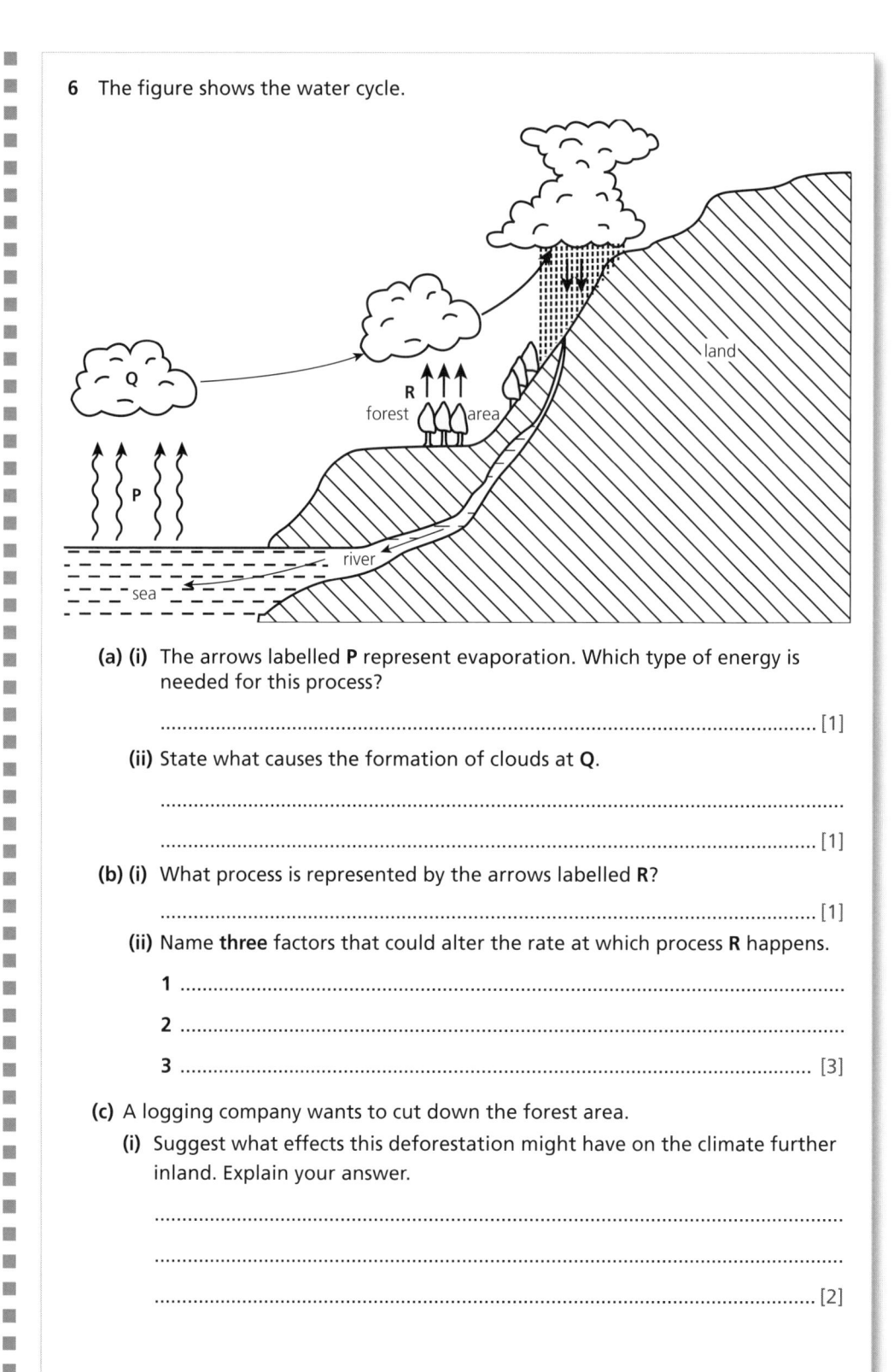

(a) (i) The arrows labelled **P** represent evaporation. Which type of energy is needed for this process?

.... [1]

(ii) State what causes the formation of clouds at **Q**.

....

.... [1]

(b) (i) What process is represented by the arrows labelled **R**?

.... [1]

(ii) Name **three** factors that could alter the rate at which process **R** happens.

1 ....

2 ....

3 .... [3]

(c) A logging company wants to cut down the forest area.

(i) Suggest what effects this deforestation might have on the climate further inland. Explain your answer.

....

....

.... [2]

(ii) State two other effects deforestation could have on the environment.

1 ....

....

2 ....

.... [2]

[Total: 10]

(Cambridge IGCSE Biology 0610, Paper 2 Q4 May/June 2009)

7 The photograph shows a root of radish covered in many root hairs.

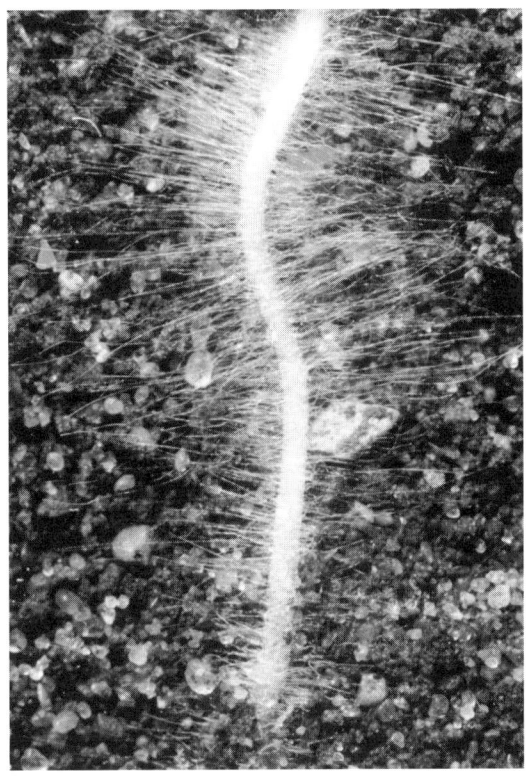

(a) Using the term *water potential*, explain how water is absorbed into root hairs from the soil.

....

....

....

....

....

.... [3]

A potometer is a piece of apparatus that is used to measure water uptake by plants.

Most of the water taken up by plants replaces water lost in transpiration.

A student used a potometer to investigate the effect of wind speed on the rate of water uptake by a leafy shoot. As the shoot absorbs water the air bubble moves upwards.

The student's apparatus is shown in the figure.

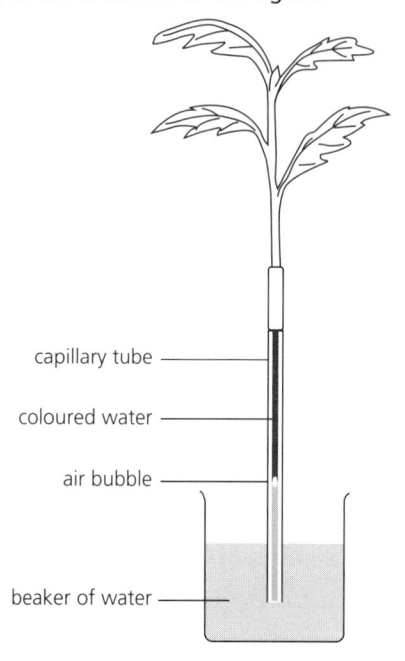

The student used a fan with five different settings and measured the wind speed. The results are shown in the table.

Wind speed / metres per second	Distance travelled by the air bubble / mm	Time / minutes	Rate of water uptake / mm per minute
0	4	10	0.4
2	12	5	2.4
4	20	5	4.0
6	35	5	7.0
8	40	2	....

(b) Calculate the rate of water uptake at the highest wind speed and write your answer in the table. [1]

(c) Describe the effect of increasing wind speed on the rate of water uptake. You may use figures from the table to support your answer.

．．． [2]

(d) State two environmental factors, **other than wind speed**, that the student should keep constant during the investigation.

1 ．．．

2 ．．．［2］

(e) Some of the water absorbed by the plants is **not** lost in transpiration. State two **other** ways in which water is used.

1 ．．．

2 ．．．［2］

(f) Water moves through the xylem to the tops of very tall trees, such as the giant redwoods of North America. The movement of water in the xylem is caused by transpiration.
Explain how transpiration is responsible for the movement of water in the xylem.

．．． ［4］

(g) Plants that live in hot, dry environments show adaptations for survival. State three **structural** adaptations of these plants.

1 ．．．

2 ．．．

3 ．．． [3]

[Total: 17]

(Cambridge IGCSE Biology 0610, Paper 31 Q4 May/June 2009)

8 The figure shows an external view of the heart and its blood vessels.

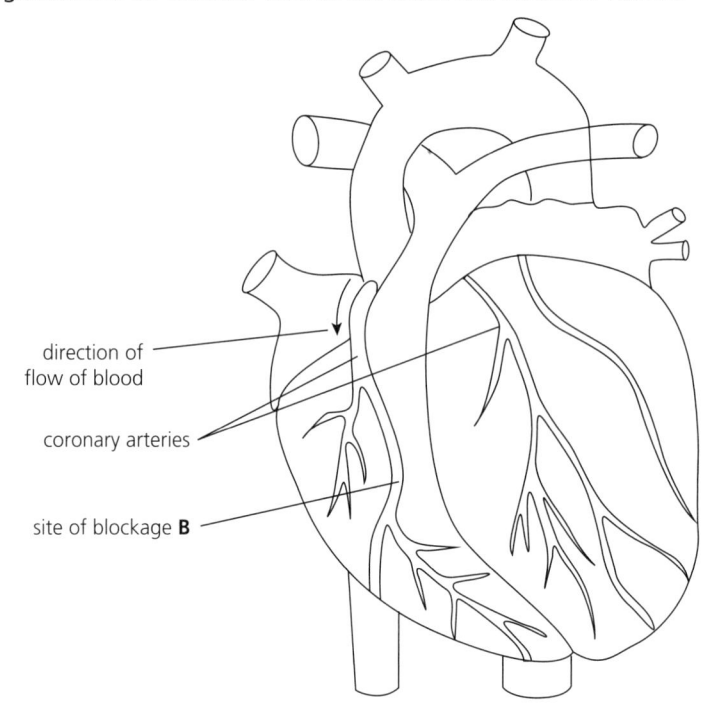

- direction of flow of blood
- coronary arteries
- site of blockage **B**

(a) The coronary arteries supply heart tissue with useful substances. Coronary veins remove waste substances.

(i) Name two useful substances the coronary arteries will supply.

1 ....

2 .... [2]

(ii) Name one waste substance the coronary veins will remove.

.... [1]

(b) The tissue forming the wall of the left ventricle responds when it is stimulated by electrical impulses.

(i) Name this type of tissue.

.... [1]

(ii) Describe how this tissue will respond when stimulated.

.... [1]

(iii) Describe the effect of this response on the contents of the left ventricle.

....

....

.... [2]

(c) The coronary arteries can become blocked with a fatty deposit, leading to a heart attack.

   (i) State two likely causes of this type of blockage.

   1 ....

   2 .... [2]

   A blockage occurs at point **B** in the coronary artery.

   (ii) On the figure shade in the parts of the artery affected by this blockage. [1]

(d) Veins have different structures from arteries.

   State two features of veins and explain how these features enable them to function efficiently.

   1 Feature ....

   ....

   Explanation ....

   ....

   2 Feature ....

   ....

   Explanation..

   .... [4]

   [Total: 14]

   (Cambridge IGCSE Biology 0610, Paper 3 Q3 Oct/Nov 2005)

9 (a) The air which is inhaled is different from that which is exhaled.

   Complete the following sentences about these differences.

   (i) Inhaled air has more .... than exhaled air. [1]

   (ii) Exhaled air has more .... and .... than inhaled air. [2]

   (iii) Inhaled air usually has a .... temperature than exhaled air. [1]

(b) One of the gases present in inhaled and exhaled air is carbon dioxide.

Describe how you could test exhaled air for carbon dioxide and describe the result if carbon dioxide is present.

Test ....

....

Result .... [2]

(c) Gases enter and leave the blood by diffusion. Define *diffusion*.

....

....

.... [2]

[Total: 8]

(Cambridge IGCSE Biology 0610, Paper 22 Q9 May/June 2010)

10 (a) Why do most waste products of metabolism have to be removed from the body?

.... [1]

(b) The figure shows the human excretory system.

Name the parts that fit each of the following descriptions.
(i) The tube that carries urine from the kidneys.

.... [1]

(ii) The organ that stores urine.

.... [1]

(iii) The blood vessel that carries blood away from the kidney.

.... [1]

(c) Outline how the kidneys remove only waste materials from the blood.

....

....

....

.... [3]

(d) Excess amino acids cannot be stored in the body and have to be broken down.
   (i) Where are excess amino acids broken down?

   .... [1]

   (ii) Which waste chemical is formed from the breakdown of excess amino acids?

   .... [1]

[Total: 9]

(Cambridge IGCSE Biology 0610, Paper 2 Q2 May/June 2009)

11 (a) The figure shows the concentration of alcohol in the blood of a person over a number of hours. During this time the person had several alcoholic drinks while eating a meal.

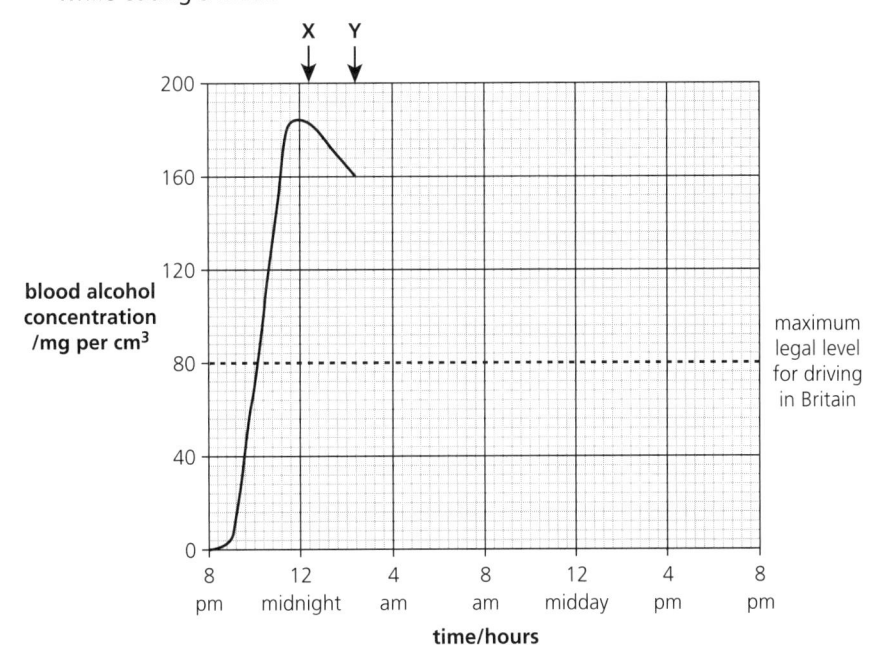

In Britain it is illegal for a person to drive a vehicle with more than 80 mg of alcohol per cm³ of blood.

(i) What is the highest concentration of alcohol in the person's blood?

..............................mg of alcohol per cm³ of blood. [1]

(ii) The alcohol in the blood is steadily broken down.
Name the organ of the body that breaks down alcohol.

.... [1]

(iii) The alcohol continues to be broken down at the same rate as between **X** and **Y**. Complete the graph, by extending the line, until there is no alcohol in the person's blood. [1]

(iv) Use the graph to predict when the person would be able to legally drive a vehicle again.

.... [1]

(b) (i) Alcohol is a depressant drug.

Explain how this could affect the ability of a person to drive a vehicle.

....

....

.... [2]

(ii) State the long-term effect alcohol can have on two named organs.

Organ 1 ....

Effect ....

Organ 2 ....

Effect .... [2]

(iii) Describe two social problems that can happen if a person becomes addicted to alcohol.

1 ....

....

2 ....

.... [2]

[Total: 10]

(Cambridge IGCSE Biology 0610, Paper 22 Q5 May/June 2010)

12 The figure shows the male reproductive system.

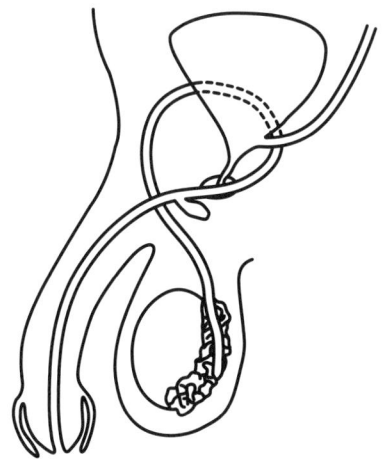

(a) Using a label line and the letters given, label on the figure:

(i) **G** where gametes are formed [1]

(ii) **S** the sperm duct [1]

(iii) **T** where testosterone is formed [1]

(iv) **U** the urethra. [1]

(b) Describe two secondary sexual characteristics regulated by testosterone.

1 ....

....

2 ....

.... [2]

(c) Choose words from the list to complete each of the spaces in the paragraph. Each word may be used once only and some words may not be used at all.

four	diploid	double	half
haploid	mitosis	meiosis	two

Gametes are formed by the division of a nucleus, a process called

.... This process produces a total of .... cells

from the original cell. Each of these cells has a nucleus described as being

.... and each nucleus contains .... the number of

chromosomes present in the original nucleus. [4]

[Total: 10]

(Cambridge IGCSE Biology 0610, Paper 2 Q8 May/June 2009)

13 A species of plant has white-flowered plants and blue-flowered plants.

If a homozygous white-flowered plant was crossed with a blue-flowered plant, all the seeds produced plants with only blue flowers.

(a) State which flower colour is controlled by the dominant allele and explain your reason for this answer.

....

.... [1]

(b) Use the symbols, **B** and **b**, to represent the two alleles for flower colours.
  (i) State the genotype of each parent plant.

   Blue-flowered plant ....

   White-flowered plant .... [2]
  (ii) State the genotype of the offspring.

   .... [1]

  (iii) Draw a genetic diagram to predict the likely results of a cross between one of the blue-flowered offspring and a white-flowered plant.

[4]

(c) The figure shows a cob of a maize plant.

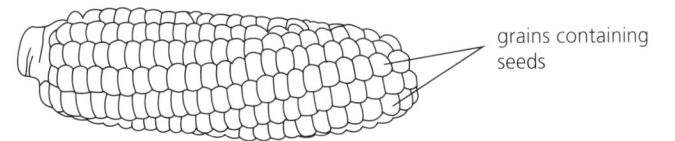

grains containing seeds

The graph shows the length of the cobs formed by a number of different maize plants. All the plants were grown from seeds from one original cob.

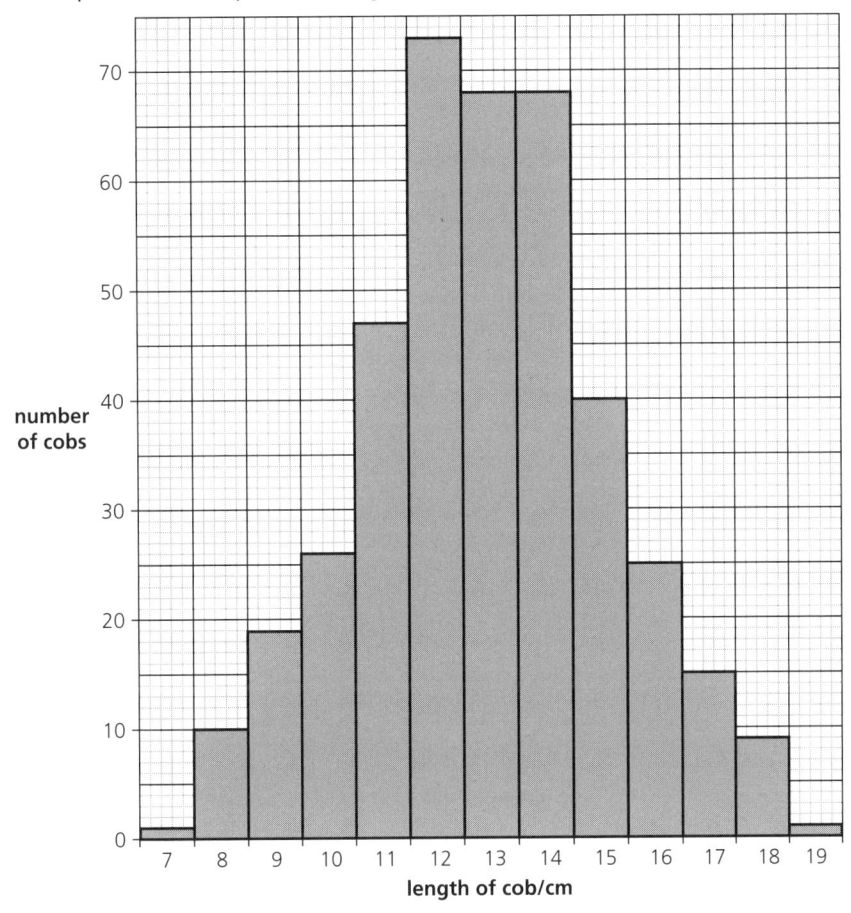

(i) Explain the evidence, visible in the graph, that shows that this is continuous variation.

....
....
.... [1]

(ii) Suggest three environmental factors that might affect the length of the maize cobs.

1 ....

2 ....

3 .... [3]

(iii) Explain how the type of variation shown by the maize cobs differs from that shown by the blue and white flowers.

....

.... [1]

[Total: 13]

(Cambridge IGCSE Biology 0610, Paper 22 Q3 May/June 2010)

14 The figure shows the processes involved in the manufacture of yoghurt.

milk
↓ ← sugar may be added
milk heat treated at 85–95 °C for 15 to 30 minutes
↓
milk homogenised to give an even consistency
↓ milk cooled
starter culture of bacteria added
↓
mixture incubated at 37–44 °C
↓ oxygen used up
↓ pH decreases
mixture cooled
↓ ← food additives and fruit added
yoghurt is packed and sent at 4 °C to shops

(a) (i) Explain why the milk must be cooled before the bacteria are added.

....

....

.... [2]

(ii) Explain why the pH decreases only **after** the oxygen in the milk has been used up.

....

....

.... [2]

(iii) Suggest **one** type of food additive that could be added to yoghurt.

.... [1]

The starter culture contains two species of bacteria, *Streptococcus thermophilus* and *Lactobacillus bulgaricus*.

The graph shows the growth of these bacteria during the production of yoghurt.

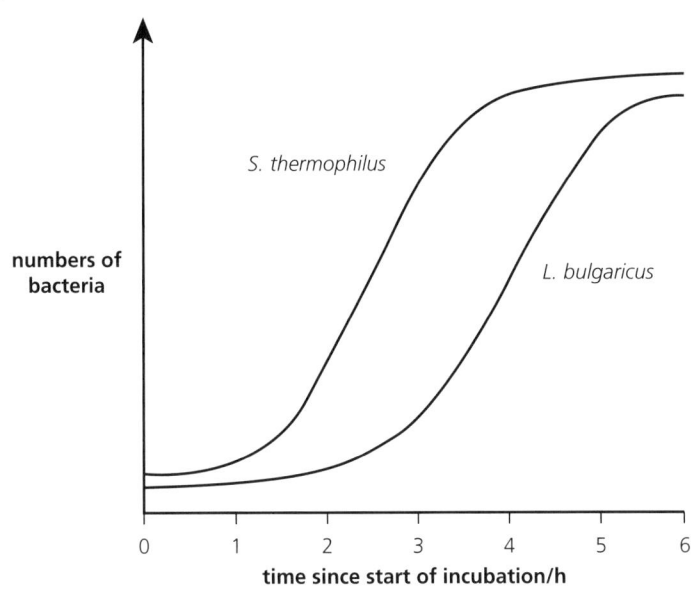

(b) Using your knowledge of population growth and the factors that affect it, describe **and** explain the growth of *S.thermophilus*, as shown in the graph.

....

....

....

....

....

....

....

....

.... [5]

(c) Suggest why the numbers of *L. bulgaricus* do not start to increase until after the increase in the numbers of *S. thermophilus*.

....

....

.... [2]

[Total: 12]

(Cambridge IGCSE Biology 0610, Paper 31 Q5 May/June 2010)

15 Acid rain is a serious environmental problem in some areas of the world. Lakes in Canada, Norway and Scotland are highly acidic as a result of acid rain.

The figure shows a cause of acid rain.

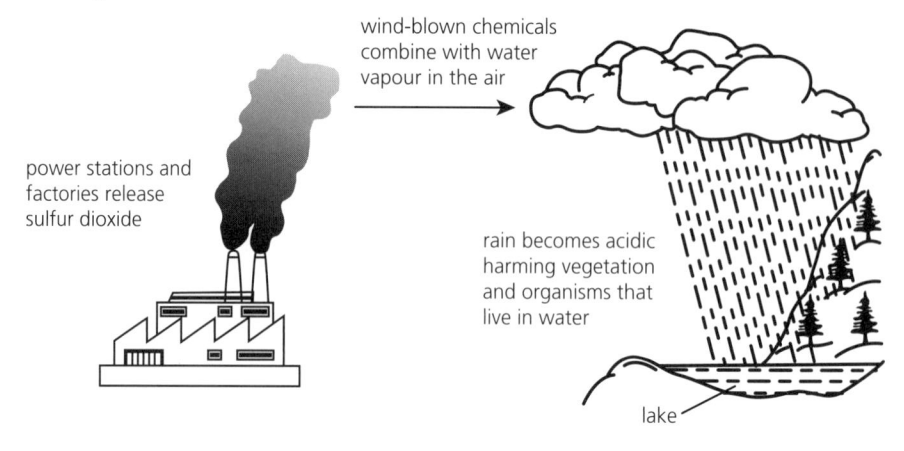

wind-blown chemicals combine with water vapour in the air

power stations and factories release sulfur dioxide

rain becomes acidic harming vegetation and organisms that live in water

lake

(a) (i) State **one** cause of acid rain **other than that shown in the figure**.

.... [1]

(ii) Describe two effects of acid rain on forest ecosystems.

1 ....

....

2 ....

.... [2]

(b) Describe two different ways to reduce pollution so that there is less acid rain.

1 ....

....

2 ....

.... [2]

The chart shows the pH ranges that some animals that live in lakes can tolerate.

animals		pH							
group	examples	7.0	6.5	6.0	5.5	5.0	4.5	4.0	3.5
fish	trout								
	bass								
	perch								
amphibians	frogs								
	salamanders								
molluscs	clams								
	snails								
crustacean	crayfish								
insects	mayfly larvae								
	blackfly larvae								

(c) State **one** feature of molluscs that is **not** a feature of crustaceans.

.... [1]

(d) Using the information in the chart above:

(i) name an animal that could be found in a lake with a pH of 4.0;

.... [1]

(ii) name the animals that are most sensitive to a decrease in pH;

.... [1]

(iii) suggest why some animals cannot tolerate living in water of pH as low as 4.0.

....

....

....

.... [2]

[Total: 10]

(Cambridge IGCSE Biology 0610, Paper 31 Q4 May/June 2010)